STORY IN MIND:
A CONSTRUCTIVIST NARRATOLOGY

The Psychological and Linguistic Foundations to How Stories Work

by

David Baboulene Ph.D.

Copyright © David Baboulene 2019

All rights reserved.

The right of David Baboulene to be identified as the author of this work has been asserted in accordance with sections 77 and 78 of the Copyright, Designs and Patents Act 1988.

www.baboulene.com

@StoryMeBad on Twitter and Facebook.

Other books by the same author:

Ocean Boulevard (2006); *Jumping Ships* (2010); *The Story Book* (2010); *Story Theory* (2014); *Story in Mind* (2019); and *The Primary Colours of Story* (2019).

No part of this book may be reproduced by any means, nor transmitted, nor translated into a machine language, without the written permission of the publisher.

Published in 2019 by DreamEngine Media Ltd.

publishing@dreamengine.co.uk

www.dreamengine.co.uk

First edition

ISBN: 978-0-9557089-7-8

Also available as an eBook.

Storytelling is not something we just happen to do. It is something we virtually have to do if we want to remember anything.

The stories we create are the memories we have.

Gerald Zaltman (2003, p.190)

Acknowledgements

To Chris Complin for his friendship, knowledge and editorial excellence.

To Thomas Pavel for his generous support and notes.

For services above and beyond the call of duty, my immense gratitude and appreciation go to my supervisors, Deborah Philips and Ewan Kirkland at the University of Brighton.

Thank you, thank you, thank you and thank you.

Table of Contents

1	**Language and Perception**	**14**
1.1	Signs, Signifiers and Signifieds	15
1.1.1	What is meaning?	17
1.2	Significations	22
1.2.1	Denotation and Connotation	26
1.3	Narrafication of the Sign	27
1.3.1	The Readerly and the Writerly	31
1.4	Narrative and Consciousness	34
1.4.1	The Protoself	35
1.4.2	The Core Self	36
1.4.3	The Autobiographical Self	36
1.4.4	Consciousness and Stories	38
1.4.5	Knowledge and Gaps	52
1.5	The Storification of the Sign	57
1.6	Summary	62
2	**A Theoretical Frame**	**66**
2.1	Information and Knowledge	66
2.2	A Constructivist Narratology	70
2.2.1	The Text	71
2.2.2	Paratext	72
2.2.3	Subtext	73
2.2.4	The Story	74
2.2.5	Syuzhet and Fabula	75
2.2.6	The Hermeneutic Boundary	79
2.2.7	Modes of Narration	80
2.3	The Theoretical Framework — Summary	83

3	**A Through-line from History**	**85**
3.1	The Rise of the Structuralist	89
3.2	Contemporary Guidance	93
3.2.1	Why Knowledge Gaps?	100
3.2.2	The Role of Structure	102
3.2.3	Subtext	109
3.3	Truth and Fiction	113
3.3.1	A STORY DEFINITION	117
3.3.2	Knowledge gaps	118
4	**A Taxonomy of Knowledge Gaps**	**120**
4.1	Rationale	122
4.2	Knowledge Gap Taxonomy	123
4.3	Classifications	124
4.3.1	Privilege and Revelation	125
4.3.2	Simple, Compound and Complex Gaps	128
4.4	Categories	129
4.4.1	Knowledge Gaps through Paratext	131
4.4.2	Paratext and Knowledge Gaps	132
4.4.3	Knowledge Gaps in Diegetic Orientation	133
4.4.4	Orientating Gaps in Mimetic Text Events	141
4.4.5	Knowledge Gaps in Text Events	150
4.4.6	Knowledge Gaps through Storification	166
5	**Case Study Recommendations**	**182**
5.1	Knowledge Gaps and Wider Applications	183
5.1.1	Knowledge Gaps and Genre	184
5.1.2	Story Industries	190

6	**Reflection and Conclusions**	**192**
6.1	Where next?	193
6.2	Conclusions	194
7	**Glossary of Terms**	**196**
8	**Bibliography**	**200**
9	**About the Author**	**206**

Notes on the text

1. In discussing a story's 'power' and the subjective evaluation of how 'good' a story is, I use the film industry rating of stories on the British Film Institute's decennial poll of critics and directors for the greatest films of all time (BFI, 2012).

2. The principles espoused in this volume are drawn primarily from film stories because of my professional background. While there are always a number of medium-specific factors, the core principles are applicable to any story in any medium.

3. This book is based upon my Ph.D. thesis, entitled: *Knowledge Gaps in Popular Hollywood Cinema: The role of information disparity in film narrative* (Baboulene, 2017). The content analysis and the knowledge gap data capture are available on my website: www.baboulene.com/clipsanddata .

4. I am conscious that there are many terms used in the early stages of this book that are not fully explained until deeper into the work. Please note, firstly, that all should become clear over time, and secondly, there is a glossary of terms in **section 7**.

Introduction

Formalism is wonderful, but narratology might also try to listen to the human heart.

(Thomas Pavel, 2017)

Although the roots of narratology date back more than 2,300 years to the time of Aristotle, the discipline really took off through the 20th century. The work of the Russian formalists was continued through the French school and from there came a global blossoming of interest. As we entered the 21st century, we had a generally accepted definition. Narratology is "the study of the logic, principles, and practices of narrative representation" (Meister, 2011). Narratologists take narratives and deconstruct them to find "narrative universals" (ibid.) and establish "the set of general statements on narrative genres, on the systematics of narrating (telling a story) and on the structure of plot" (Ryan & von Alphen 1993: 110).

However, along with narratology's rapid formalisation has come a persistent frustration. These 'systematics' and 'the structure of plot', as well as the more compelling 'narrative universals', have generally suffered from damning exceptions. Terms that narratology should own and understand, such as 'subtext', 'genre' and even the term 'story' have escaped singular definition. This creates an uncertainty at the very basis of narratology, which is compounded when the term 'narrative' is used by other disciplines in their work. Cognitive psychology, sociology, neuroscience, education, legal, religious, political and medical discourse each apply their own context to the terms 'narration' and 'story', and these rarely sit in harmony with the context and terminology offered by narratology. As narratologists, what we do is not as useful or applicable as it should be. Even in the commercial world of story industries and entertainment, the guidance given to those who create and invest in stories carries that same frustration captured by Thomas Pavel in the quotation above; that narratology does not quite do the job that they would like it to do.

I argue that we cannot claim to have appropriately formalised narratology until the terms and definitions we use ourselves and which we offer to the world, firstly, have no popular exceptions and, secondly, are readily and usefully applicable to any discipline that uses the terms we claim to understand. For a valid essentialist stance to emerge, narratology must find a basis that is true to its story roots. We must find an approach to stories which does not require us to be satisfied with the limitations of 'narrative representation', because a story is more than the structures in the text. A story is a communication between an author and a receiver of story, not a communication between a text and a receiver. A story is psychological at its source and at its reception. It is only in transit between the author and the receiver that it has recognisable 'systematics of narrating (telling a story)' or any 'structure of plot' (ibid.). Narratology is a social science and it applies to an art form. Narratology must be readily applicable to all the areas in which we know intuitively that narrative is in play; the cognitive, affective, motivational, behavioural, political and ethical.

In this book, I argue that narratology, by beginning with a text and a process of analysis that seeks 'systematics', 'structures' and 'narrative universals' (ibid.) is starting from the wrong place. Narratology is beginning from the *result* of the process of narrative creation, not from the source. It is this that turns us into structuralists from the outset. We are immediately working with the structure of existing texts, and we have ruled out the human heart, the mental dynamics and creative processes.

This has led us into a somewhat warped logic. Imagine a study of every genius that ever lived. A structuralist might arrive at the conclusion that, because every genius that has ever lived possessed a skeleton, the skeleton can be seen to be the substance of genius. This is very difficult to argue against. The statistics are highly convincing. At the practical level, if you remove the skeleton from a genius they do not seem half so clever any more. With such a compelling base, the structuralist keeps ploughing on, searching for the substance of genius through ever-deeper investigations into the nature of skeletons and the implied correlation with genius. Now, this is a little glib, of course, but I argue that narratology has been tricked along these lines. A narrative structure is an inevitable *consequence* of creating a story so narratology has devoted itself to analysing the structure of texts. There is clear correlation between skeletons and genius... but there is no causation. In the same way that a structuralist becoming an expert on skeletons will never truly establish the substance of genius, so a structuralist becoming an expert on narrative representations in existing texts implicitly excludes the creator and their mind, the receiver and their mind, and, indeed, as we shall see, they are also excluding *the story*. Narratology recognises the narrative and has the tools to uncover its structure, but there is a difference between a narrative and a story, and it is at this fundamental junction that narratology sets its scope too narrow. In this book I intend to show how narratology is a discipline concerned exclusively with narrative, and a discipline that, by its own definition, excludes story.

This work will demonstrate how story and narrative are separated by the same gulf that exists between the skeleton and the mind of a genius. Or, if you prefer, between the structuralism at the heart of orthodox narratology and the subjective qualities of stories. While it can be argued that narratology is wise to avoid the deep subjective waters involved in the psychology of story — the author's mindset, the receiver's activities and so on — it is equally a fundamental flaw of narratology if it does not embrace story.

Pierre Macherey stated that: "No description of the conventions of reading, however thorough, can replace a theory of literary production" (Macherey, 1966, p.73). For narratology to find its true roots, it must broaden. It must include meaning as well as structure. Knowledge as well as information. The human as well as the text. This implies a constructivist discipline; that is, one that recognises the need for a human mind to be included to give meaning to narrative.

The purist will be relieved to know that a constructivist approach does not dismiss the orthodoxy but builds on the wisdom that is already there. It broadens the canvas for narratology, retaining the structuralist imperatives and existing narratological foundations but with an acceptance that a text is never merely a text. The text has an originator (a human mind) and it must be interpreted by a receiver of that text (another human mind) for it to have meaning. This work will extend the understanding of narrative to include the human minds that give the narrative meaning and include the psychological dynamics that encode a story into a text and decode that text back into a story.

This is a tricky balancing act, because at no point in this work will I attempt to specify the mindset of either the author or the receiver of a story. I shall create a model whereby it is possible to identify the cues planted by the author into the text, but I will not claim to know what they are thinking. I will also identify the triggers that will inspire a response in the receiver of a text, but again, I will not attempt to specify what the receiver thinks as a result. The cues and triggers are objective and tangible, however the mindsets at the point of cause and effect will not be specified.

This book sets out with the following aims:

1) To present a narratology based on a constructivist approach. The result will embrace traditional structuralist values but will broaden narratology to include mental processes at the source of story creation and the related and unavoidable phenomenology of story reception. That is, a narratology built not on the text, but on the dynamics between the author and the receiver of the story; dynamics that are *evident* in the text.

    Using these mental dynamics, the book presents a narratology that situates the text as a facilitator of the conversation between the author and the receiver. The conversation, not just the medium, is meaningful to narratology. I will therefore hypothesise a set of dynamics integral to the text which trigger the exchange of knowledge and meaning between the author and the receiver. These dynamics will form the roots of a constructivist narratology.

2) To demonstrate how this narratology encompasses any and every story, irrespective of media, genre, duration, ethnicity or age. Additionally, to extend the scope of narratology to render it applicable beyond the domain of story industries. An essentialist narratology that is relevant and useful to all other disciplines that wish to use and apply terms such as 'story' and 'narrative' to their own context and requirements.

In this book, I have selected those elements of story theory, neuroscience, linguistics and semiology that come together to make a constructivist narratology comprehensive enough to satisfy the narratological purist, but which also delivers a cohesive set of terms and definitions to allow 'narrative' and 'story' to be explored and defined beyond the limits of textual representation. A narratology that unites the writer and their process, the text and its analysis, the narration and its media, the receiver and some specified dynamics of reception. A narratology that begins with the creator of a story, not the text, and embraces human narrative mental processes as well as the structure of the text. A framework that unifies all uses of the term 'narrative'.

No pressure then! Let's get started. And let's begin at the beginning.

1   Language and Perception

There can be no human consciousness without a system of signs.

Mikhail Bakhtin (1895 – 1975)

(Quoted in Eagleton, 2008, p.102)

According to Heather Whipps (2008), around 250,000 years ago (although there is much debate over this timing), an apparently innocent change took place in the throat architecture of early *homo sapiens*. All hominids have a small bone in the throat called the hyoid bone. It is the only bone in the body that is not connected to any other bones. As *homo sapiens* became more upright over time, gravity got to work on the hyoid bone. Its position in the upper front of the throat articulated relative to a descending larynx... and the planet was changed forever.

Whereas our earlier ancestors were capable of a range of sounds comparable to other hominids (such as those produced by a chimpanzee), this small change in throat architecture enabled suitably endowed *homo sapiens* to produce complex sounds. Complex sounds allowed them to work together more effectively and the more sophisticated their range of sounds became, the more sophisticated became their ability to cooperate. The more their language developed, and the more sophisticated the cooperation became, the more complex and organised their relationships became, and the roots of what we call 'civilisation' were put down. Civilisation can be seen as cooperation taken to its logical extreme, and language is the key that allowed it all to happen (cf., Whipps, 2008).

In this chapter, I am going to look at the evolution of language in the form of the four stages of linguistic mental processing necessary as a framing for stories. The chapter also proposes a relationship between mental processes that deal with real-life scenarios compared with the same processes when receiving a fictional narrative.

The four stages we will look at are:

Signs (the basic unit of communication through language)

Significations (the cultural meaning of a sign for the receiving individual)

Narrafications (signs and significations plus change over time)

Storifications (the meaning of a narrafication for the receiving individual).

You may already know much of the foundational material regarding signs and significations, however the concepts of narrafication and storification are my own. In discussing these concepts, the chapter provides a through-line of logic that builds from linguistics to story and leads to conclusions and material you are unlikely to have met before. I recommend you read the material you already know in order to slide smoothly into the material that is new.

1.1 Signs, Signifiers and Signifieds

The study of signs and symbols is known as semiology, pioneered by the Swiss linguist Ferdinand de Saussure (1857-1913) in the late 1800s. Saussure invites us to consider a train. In itself, a train is a solid, real object we can point at and agree upon, and we would generally use the same language and terms to identify it. Train. But what about 'The 8.15 Geneva to Paris' train? What makes *that* train the 8.15 Geneva to Paris train? Is it the train itself? The locomotive? The carriages? No, it can't be, because none of the practical, physical things that define today's '8.15 to Paris' were there yesterday, and they will be different again tomorrow. Is it the people? The driver? The passengers? No. They change too. Is it the time it leaves the station? There is a good chance it won't even leave at 8.15 (it certainly would not if it was a British train...). Besides, if it leaves at 9.45 we will still be calling it the 8.15. Who labelled it? Well, some people who run the railways decide that a train will leave at a certain time, and that becomes the reference for that specific train. Right. It must be the timetable and the management. But we are pointing at a train, and that is all office-based paperwork and planning. We are losing our focus on the object. So, what makes 'the 8.15 Geneva to Paris' a type of train?

In his ground-breaking *Course in General Linguistics* (Saussure, 1916), Saussure separated the labels given to objects (the 'signifier') from the meanings they generate in mind (the 'signified') and called the two taken together a linguistic 'sign'.

Figure 1 - 'Bear' as a sign

A stimulus to the senses — the signifier — triggers a mental concept in mind, the signified, and the two taken together comprise a complete linguistic sign. Which of the three components of the linguistic sign defines the communication, and gives it *meaning*?

1. **The Signifier**

    The label we all agree upon (the signifier) for the concept of a bear is a variable. A different convention could just as easily have been adopted for our communication. For example, the signifier **αρκούδα** will stimulate an equivalent mental concept in a Greek speaker as the signifier **bear** does to an English speaker. So, the signifier is not the key in defining our communication. As long as all communicators agree it, then it does not matter what it is. It's a variable, and therefore cannot be the defining component of a linguistic communication.

2. **The Referent**

   The referent is the item in the real world that the sign indicates — in this case an actual bear. Again, this cannot be the defining component of the linguistic exchange because it is not necessarily present at the moment of communication and it does not need to be present for language to be useful. Indeed, as we shall see, many of the referents used in language have no material existence. They only exist as linguistic concepts in mind. A 'Sunday', a 'Marriage', 'Summer' or 'Economics' only have a presence in mind, and no tangible presence in the real world. In linguistics, the referent is not the defining element of a communication.

3. **The Signified**

   So it must be the signified; the concept spawned in mind as a result of interpreting the signifier. Clearly this does not exist tangibly in the real world either. It only manifests as a phenomenological structure in mind. (In semiology 'phenomena' are the mental representations of experience.) Even for the simplest of signs the signified must be an interpretation, and this can lead to differences that depend upon the receiver. For example, as you can see, my friend in figure 1 got a grizzly bear from the signifier BEAR, whereas you might get a Polar bear, someone else might get a koala and someone else might think I meant a teddy bear. And all along I meant a pessimist in the stock market. And this is the simplest of signs. The signified is therefore also a variable that depends upon the receiver's knowledge, experience, mindset and the context in which the sign is presented. The signified is therefore not the defining element of linguistic communication either.

All of which means that a linguistic sign comprises three intangibles. It is a circle of uselessness, with each only having sense when the other two are present. It takes all three to work together to create **meaning**. And meaning is what we are after. So, the question becomes:

1.1.1 What is meaning?

Meaning requires two further components. Firstly, it requires a *system*. Each sign is set in a context set by other signs — the system of signs to which this sign belongs. A mental understanding of a linguistic sign is only *meaningful* in terms of the sign-structures of which it is a component and, of course, each of these structures is also a mental object. In the system of signs called 'language', to explain the meaning of one word, I have to use other words. There's no other way. If I say 'bear' and add another sign, say, 'Australia', now we are more likely to find a majority generating a koala bear as a signified. If we take the sign 'bear' and add the sign 'Arctic', now we are more likely to generate a signified Polar bear. This happens because the context provided by other signs helps to give meaning to this one.

To clarify this, Saussure invites us to consider a chess piece. By itself, it is a meaningless trinket. It is not meaningful until we place it within the context of (the 'language' of) chess. Now, through mutual agreement amongst those who understand and share the language of chess, the piece has significance. By agreeing the meaning of a chess piece, that is, creating a system and setting its place in that system, people can share its value in the context of chess. Can you replace a knight with, say, a biscuit, and still play chess? Yes, of course. Because it is not the signifier that is important, it is the chess piece's relative role in the system — and in the minds of the chess playing community who share the sign system — that gives a context to the knight (or biscuit) in relation to the other pieces and the rules of the game. What makes a sign meaningful is, firstly, its uniqueness in comparison to all other signs (it is only valid if it is different from all other signs in this particular system) and, secondly, how it is situated in terms of the mental sub-structures (signs) it is 'made from' and the meta-structures (signs) of which it is a component.

A knight only makes sense in terms of its differences to the king, queen, pawn, castle and bishop, and its individual functions in the language of chess. The signifieds/significations for each of these things exist only in mind, can only be given meaning in a context of each other and form a complete language of chess through providing the set of concepts that define everything that comprises chess.

> The language of chess is a system of signs that exists only in mind and makes sense only in terms of the other signs in the system.

> The language of human communication is a system of signs that exists only in mind and makes sense only in terms of the other signs in the system.

As an aside, my son (age 10) used the word 'blom' in an argument the other day. I said: 'Hold on! You can't get away with that. That word is made up!'

He looked me in the eye and said: 'All words are made up.'

And he is right. A word is just a word. 'BLOM'. It is only meaningful if it can be structured into a mental map of signs which frame it in a human context. We can only define a word by using other words. It is only these other words that give meaning to this one, and each of those words has a meaning that can only be communicated using words. A dictionary is a complete set of words, the meanings of which are defined using other words. If you don't know the meaning of the word 'dictionary', you have to look it up... in a dictionary.

My son then dunked my knight in his tea, ate it and proudly announced: 'Check mate.'

Is Anybody There?

Which brings us to the second requirement for meaning: a human mind. Several times in the above text, I said that X, Y or Z 'exists only in mind'. This is because human meaning, logically enough, requires a human mind. This may seem obvious, but it is well worth mentioning. Philosophically, I am a constructivist, and the philosophical foundation of this research is constructivism. The fundamental premise for constructivism is the philosophical acceptance that there is a real world, but that *meaning* only exists if there is a human mind to give it that meaning. Realists assert that the world exists independently of the human mind, therefore everything we can ever know has its provable basis in the real world. Idealists, on the other hand, believe everything we know can only ever be in mind. They are sceptical about how much can ever be known about anything that is mind-independent, even to the extent of denying the existence of a mind-independent world.

Constructivism is a philosophical perspective that does not isolate reality from the mind. It implicitly links the two. As Michael Crotty states:

> According to constructivists the world is independent of human minds, but knowledge of the world is always a human and social construction. [...] Truth, or meaning, comes into existence in and out of [one's] engagement with the realities in [one's] world. There is no meaning without a mind. Meaning is not discovered but constructed. In this understanding of knowledge it is clear that different people may construct meaning in different ways, even in relation to the same phenomenon. In this view of things, subject and object emerge as partners in the generation of meaning. (Crotty, 1998, p.1-17)

I shall be building a constructivist narratology. In this context, **phenomena** are the structures of meaning we build in mind as a result of experience, and we build these phenomena out of signs. I know this is a lot to take in, but fear not, these things will clarify as we go along. For the moment, the key distinction to make is that **information** is the stimulation of our senses from items and events in the real world, but **knowledge** and **meaning** are solely constructed in mind. This is a critical distinction: There is no knowledge outside of the mind. No knowledge 'out there'. Knowledge is purely in mind. This is why there is no meaning to a narrative without a human being present to give it meaning. The human receives information from the outside world and interprets it into knowledge in mind. More on this later.

A system of signs

We build a galaxy of concepts through language (that is, a system of signs), each of which makes sense in terms of the others in the system. It is important to recognise how critical this is. It is this linguistic system, structured into knowledge, which makes human beings exceptional, and defines the nature of our peculiarly human existence. But we are getting ahead of ourselves. From what we have so far, what is it that makes this particular train the 8.15 Geneva to Paris train? In the context that has been expounded, it is two things: the differences from other signs in the same linguistic system, and the context relative to the other signs in the system:

1) **Differences.** In the language of train travel, it must be the explicable differences of this train from all other trains; that is, it is the meaning of the words we use ("the 8.15 from Geneva to Paris") that differentiate it in the language of train travel. It is the time and the points of departure and destination that *give it meaning* in the context of human knowledge. Train engineers do not use the language of travel; they have a different system and a different context. Engineers do not fix 'the 8.15 Geneva to Paris' train — they do not know or care where it goes or when. The engineers fix the one with differences to other trains in the context of *the language of* train engineering.

2) **Relative Context.** The train's context in the system of signs that make up the language of train travel give it meaning. That is, how this train is situated in a phenomenological knowledge context in mind. To understand the meaning of 'the 8.15 Geneva to Paris' train, it is necessary to build a concept in your mind from your existing knowledge of (the language of) time, the function and use of trains as a form of transport and the concepts involved in personal travel (tickets, timetable, money, connections, and so on).

By taking one sign — BEAR — and adding one more — AUSTRALIA — the meaning of 'bear' was changed and refined. However, we normally add dozens and dozens to create a concept and clarify a meaning. The system is a galaxy of signs, so 'the 8.15 Geneva to Paris' train is situated in a variety of relevant phenomenological concepts, all of which must be understood and brought together to make human sense of 'the 8.15 Geneva to Paris' train.

Ok. So far so good. Signs are composed from a signifier/signified pair. Signs are the fundamental unit of constructivist phenomena (mental models of experience) that situate concepts as knowledge and give them meaning. Signs are fundamental to thinking. However, you and I know that we do not think in signs. So what else is going on?

1.2 Significations

Roland Barthes (1915 – 1980) built on Saussure's advances in linguistics and semiology. Amongst much noteworthy work, he came up with the concept of **signification**, consolidated in his 1957 work, *Mythologies* (1957). Signification is achieved through a specific manipulation of the linguistic sign, whereby the complete sign we depicted earlier (a first level sign) becomes a signifier for a second level 'signification' that includes the signified's cultural meaning over and above its simple, denoted meaning. Take the basic, first level sign: FLOWER. This may inspire a context — a constructed set of signifieds in mind — for what 'flower' means to you. Perhaps it makes you think of botany, a greenhouse, seeds, bulbs, Kew Gardens, pots, earth, petals, stamens, bees, pollination and so on.

Now, the key words in that paragraph are: 'What this means to you'. As Crotty said in the earlier quote: 'In this understanding of knowledge it is clear that different people may construct meaning in different ways, even in relation to the same phenomenon.' (Crotty, 1998, p.1-17). And this is critical to all that follows. Because, as you grow up and learn through experience of life and culture, so the meaning of a sign changes. When you add your personal knowledge and experience, the sign transforms, because the mind overlays a meaning inherited through cultural use of that same sign. It involves the sign being appropriated as a whole and treated as a signifier for a new sign. This sign is created not only from stimulation to the senses, but from correlating that stimulation with knowledge in mind. If the sign 'flower' is contextualised within a bouquet and a cake with candles, it signifies a celebration; perhaps a birthday. If it is contextualised on the logo of a sports team, for people with the relevant knowledge and experience it will signify the English national rugby team.

This is known as the appropriation of the sign, whereby it is emptied of its basic meaning and bequeathed a new meaning through a cultural overlay. These must be learned, just as the signifier 'flower' and its signified had to be learned in the first place, and they become a new form of 'truth' in the way the sign is constructed. If we situate a flower culturally, in the context of other signs, such as 'coffin', 'hearse', 'priest', 'grave' and 'cemetery', a new and powerful signification is evident to us to do with death and grieving. Signs in the language of funerals. The basic sign is gone. Replaced. Botany, earth, petals and bees are long forgotten, the flowers signifying death and mourning. The fact that this is all linguistic, and exists only in the mind of a person, and is only there in that person's mind at all because society put it there, shows how it is possible to overlay new values and qualities derived from the sign-as-signifier.

Signification is a function of the qualities that are embedded in mind through learning and experience. From your earliest exposures to the sign 'flower', in films, conversations, education, marketing, portrayal in media, and in the words, ideas, rhetoric and reactions of those around you, you learn to overlay a set of values in how you interpret a 'flower' that is dependent upon the cultural context and your recognition and understanding of that cultural context. When you become capable of this (that is, you have learned the cultural significance), you automatically empty out the signified of the first level sign and populate the signifier of the second level 'signification'.

Here is a sign — 'flower':

Figure 2 - Signification

What comes to mind? Botany? Earth? Pollination? Death? Birthdays?! Not at all. Anyone with appropriate cultural understanding empties the signified into a new second level signifier, and receives in mind a signification concerned with love, romance and courtship.

By taking the reality of the sign and overlaying new meaning drawn from our culture, we move from denotation (the first level truth of flowers in nature) to connotation (meaning received in mind **via our personal knowledge, history and cultural experience**), and we receive 'flowers' — the signification. Notice how we make a *direct* and instantaneous association between the sign 'rose' and the qualities we have been invited to associate with it throughout our lives, to do with love, romance and courtship. This is an unavoidable reflex and it is knowledge. If we think it, it is a form of truth, because it is how society teaches us to understand the signifier. One could say that it is not just the signifier that is appropriated, it is our mind!

Advertisers think along these lines all the time. When you see a deodorant brand and you somehow feel its use will make you irresistible to the opposite sex; when you see an alcoholic drink and you think its consumption will bring you an endearingly mischievous personality; when you see a cleaning fluid and you think its use will save your family from death at the hands of 99% of all known germs, you are being trained to override the first level signifier (in reality, it is a smell/poison/detergent...), empty it out and fill it with signification. You've bought the myth; and because you unconsciously interpret every single sign you see, it becomes a powerful form of truth in the world, even when you know it is happening and even when you make a conscious effort to resist. The receiver of this signification must have cultural knowledge and prior understanding of how society uses this sign in order to create the myth for themselves; but create it they will, and even the most cynical of receivers — those who deny that they are susceptible and refuse to accept that the myth has entered their brain — will receive the signification and its meaning. (They must do, or they would not be in a position to reject it!)

This isn't just marketing; this is meaning in language. And it isn't simply coercive and negative (although it is easy to focus on the cynical side). There are innumerable significations we derive from our cultural understanding throughout our daily lives; indeed, they *define* our cultural understanding.

Myth

In *Mythologies*, Barthes analyses the function of a set of significations from popular culture and journalism, overlaying the receiver's history and knowledge on to the signified, thereby delivering a political message through connotation. This is what he called a myth, or "second order semiotic signification" (Barthes, 1957, p.113). While mythology is a story tradition in mainstream usage, in Barthes' terms, a myth is the meaning in mind planted through signification. Barthes's principal example is a magazine cover which shows a black soldier saluting the French flag. At the level of first-order semiotics, this image is a signifier which denotes a soldier saluting a flag. But at the second-order mythological level, it signifies the idea of France as a great, multi-ethnic empire, an imperial force loved by its colonies.

Barthes looked at wine. As a signified, it is an alcoholic drink. However, through widely shared signification, the French perceive wine as sustenance for the worker; it brings a sharper mind to the intellectual; in winter it warms; in summer it cools and refreshes. Barthes argues that in France wine is never linked with intoxication, violence or crime (Barthes, 1957, p.58–61). For the French, and through signification, wine equates to strong, positive French identity. To drink wine is to be proudly French, irrespective of any knowledge of the true damage done by alcohol. "To believe in wine is a coercive collective act" (Barthes, 1957, p.59). Myth takes an object and transforms it into the sign of a universal value; in this case, a collective French identity. Signification and myth are the building blocks of rhetoric.

Just about everything signifies to some extent and with varying levels of innocence. Language is made from signs and symbols, so this sort of mental reflex rightly happens in our minds all the time. Indeed, most of our thinking involves interpretation and the *meaning* we derive is abstracted away from the simple, denoted nature of solid items and events we can predict and rely upon in the real world. We do not simply see an object and think one real-world truth about it. We construct a meaning around the signifiers, situate them within a context of other stimuli and signs, turn the signifieds into new significations, broaden them into a narrative set of events-over-time, construct concepts made from concepts, and arrive at something a great deal more complex than the simple truth of the original signifier. For constructivists, there is no **knowledge** in nature. Knowledge is only in mind and everything has an extension to its existence in terms of what it means to a human mind. The truth of an object or event is not the simple matter of its being. That is only information. The complete truth of an object or event is in its phenomenology; what it means once it is interpreted into knowledge in mind. It is in this distinction that I can perhaps go some way to answering one of the great philosophical questions: 'If a tree falls in the forest and there is nobody there to hear it, does it make a sound?' My answer is that it does not make a *meaningful* sound, because for an action to have meaning, there must be a human being present to perceive it and interpret it into knowledge in mind.

1.2.1 Denotation and Connotation

These terms will come up many times and provide a useful distinction, so let us take a moment to clarify them.

Denotation occurs when there is an unambiguous relationship between information and the knowledge it triggers into mind. If I write the word 'car', and you receive a phenomenological entity in mind that is, simply and fundamentally, a car, this is denotation. The primary, implicit meaning of the word. Nothing clever or abstract, a simple one-to-one link between the signifier and the signified. Thus, 'rose' denotes 'flower'.

Connotation requires some form of cultural knowledge and understanding to derive meaning from the signifier that is abstracted away from the denoted meaning of information. Thus 'James Bond Car' connotes knowledge in mind that involves cultural meaning over and above a denoted 'car'. 'The cat sat on the mat' is denoted information; however 'the cat sat on the dog's mat' inspires connotation for people who understand the relationship between cats and dogs. The signifier 'rose' denotes 'flower'; whereas it connotes 'romance'.

As you can see, the leap from a basic sign to a culturally embedded, mind-altering myth is quite something, but this is just the start. From here, things really accelerate, because, as I intimated earlier, our minds do not work just with objects, simple signifiers and their signifieds, and not even with significations. Our minds work with **events** and must accommodate a fourth dimension: continuous change over time. This implies two further mental dynamics which I have coined the **narrafication** and the **storification** of the sign.

1.3   Narrafication of the Sign

So far, we have discussed relatively static signs and their associated significations — bear, train, flower, car and so on. However, we do not hold objects in mind in these discrete, itemised ways like a computer does. Try to explain the concept of a 'daughter' without any context provided by other signs, such as female and male, father and mother, family, brother, genetics, and things become very difficult. Linguistic communication is a system that creates "a galaxy of signifiers [...] forming 'nebulae' of signifieds" (Barthes, 1990, pp.4,8). And that is before we add the most important and complicating factor of all: change over time.

When an association is made between objects in mind, it is often their role in the context of change over time that gives them full meaning. A bear, train, flower or car is meaningful in terms of what it *does* in relation to other signs in the system, not what it *is*. A train is meaningful in terms of the journey you wish to make. A rose is meaningful in terms of an unfolding romance. If you are having a picnic in Yellowstone Park, now a bear becomes meaningful in wholly different ways from the static signifier of figure 1. With the addition of change over time, the processing that is going on in your mind to interpret and give meaning to the myriad of signs and significations assaulting your senses now includes the changing relationships between them — the narrafications — that represent *events*. Stories are made from **action** and actions combine to create events. Events are signifiers too (made from signs) and events are significations as well, and these too can be connected by interactions — change over time — within them. A bullet is a sign, and a signification. Loading a bullet into a gun is an event that signifies. Two soldiers fighting represents an event, as does the battle they are part of, as is the war of which that battle is one of many. It is possible to abstract out all the smaller component signs and significations and replace them with a single narrafication that constitutes all the detail without knowing or particularly needing to know about the components that created it. We understand a football match, or a war, or a marriage, or a holiday or an entire period in history as a sign, with perhaps a defining quality, such as the result or outcome, but with little or no detail beyond that. We can then treat this event as an object — a sign — in its own right. This is also important in the practical matter of holding so much information in mind. You may well remember an event, such as a 'holiday to Italy' or 'My 18th birthday' with no detail, and yet you can choose to drill down into the detail by dividing the event up into its component events at any time that the detail is triggered.

Narrafication is not simply adding an exponentially increasing quantity of signs and significations to the assault on the receiver's senses. There are two further elements that accumulate atop the signs and significations. Firstly, an event is a new sign or signification in itself. The interaction of signs and significations creates a meaning that is a function of that change over time. The impact of one set of signs upon another through interaction brings new meaning that is different from the constituent parts. There would be no battle and no war if there was no change over time, and the overall meaning of the narrafication 'war' additionally manifests at a whole different level in international politics. Narrafication also brings **causal logic**. Things happen for a reason. Narrative is change over time, in the sense of actions that create a cause-effect chain. Note that events happen (change over time happens) continuously in nature irrespective of the presence of a human being. However, there must be a human perceiver present for a narrative event to be meaningful. Narrafication is the process of a human perceiver converting narrative events into meta-signs incorporating causal human logic in mind. True understanding is generally only possible upon completion of the delivery of all the relevant information that constitutes a complete event. With change over time, meaning comes from an understanding of the signs, significations *and* narrafications that together comprise that entire event.

It is important to note how narrafications are built out of knowledge. Whilst signs and significations place a phenomenological entity into mind that may have a cultural overlay, when you add change over time it is no longer a one-to-one relationship with an object. It's an ever-changing *narrative* meaning that is built from the signs, significations and narrafications that are drawn together into a greater entity bonded through human causal logic.

This seems like a good time to nail down some definitions. **An event** is an action or series of actions, and **a narrative** is an event or a series of events comprising change over time. It does not have to educate anyone or entertain or even be interesting. As long as there is change over time, it is a narrative. Every day, all over the galaxy, things change, and when change over time is linked by cause and effect, it is a narrative. Somewhere in the cosmos, a spider is spinning a web; a moon is eclipsing a sun; a tree is falling in a forest; birds of paradise are dancing their courtship. All of these are narratives, as is any *representation* of change over time, for example through storytelling. However, a narrative does not become meaningful until there is a human mind to perceive it. Why? Because this is philosophy. Human thinking and consciousness are the basis of knowledge and philosophy, and in a constructivist epistemology, there is no meaning without a human mind to make that meaning. Meaning is knowledge, and knowledge is only in mind. There is no knowledge in nature. As we shall see in the next section, narratives, as phenomenological constructs in mind, are a defining substance of human consciousness. So, for a narrative to have meaning, there must be a human mind present to convert the information that is inherent in the narrative and stimulating the senses of a receiving person into structured human knowledge in mind.

Events of change over time happen continuously. Narrafication is the process of correlating events into story in mind. An event is a narrative, but it is not a meaningful narrative unless there is a human present to receive it and interpret it into a story in mind.

A narration is the real-time delivery of a narrative. Irrespective of medium or form, duration or intent — when a narrative is delivered to the senses of a human receiver, narration is the act of communication. A narration is an information stream, and everything that goes into that information stream during the real-time delivery becomes part of the narration. There is a lot to be said about what is included in a narration, for example, the knowledge you have of a film star's private life can be part of a film narration, as might the information in the film's marketing or poster. This is all information contributing to the story that is built in mind. I was at a screening recently, during which a lady in the screening room fainted and fell down some stairs. The screening continued, but her fall became part of the narration (whether we wanted it to or not) because it became part of the information stream. Yes, it was incongruous in terms of the causal logic, but it happened, it changed the nature and form of audience engagement in the story. It was part of the experience for the receivers of the narration, and therefore became part of the story in mind. For the moment, the narration is a real-time delivery of a narrative to a human receiver.

We could run a film with no audience. This would be an event — a screening event — however, as a narration it would be meaningless. Like the tree falling in the forest, narrative communication of this form is not *meaningful* unless there is a human receiver present to interpret it into a meaningful knowledge instead of just an information stream.

A story. At this early stage, the main thing to recognise in terms of a definition is that a story is only ever found inside the mind of a human being. The narration is the specific, real-time telling of a narrative; and receiving the narration inspires (a version of) that narrative to be produced in the mind of the receiver. This unique *production* of the narrative in mind is the story. 'The cat sat on the mat' is a narrative (it is an event with change over time) and once you have understood that narrative, and built the phenomenological structures to represent that narrative in mind, that is the story. It may not be a very *good* story, but change over time, represented phenomenologically as causal logic in mind, is a story.

Narrafication. This is the process of interpreting signs and signifiers into not just significations, but narratives in mind (story) that include change over time and interactions between events, objects and the relationships between them. Narrafication is the conversion of narrative information assaulting the senses into phenomenological narrative in mind.

Narrative and story

At this point, a statement I have touched on once or twice can be clarified. When Pavel tells us that "Formalism is wonderful, but narratology might also try to listen to the human heart" (Pavel, 2017), my explanation for his plaintive call is that narratology focuses exclusively on narrative. That is, on the information stream that assaults the senses. For narratology to be comprehensive and useful, it must also embrace story. Narratology, as "the study of the logic, principles, and practices of narrative representation"

(Meister, 2011) "narrative universals" and "the systematics of narrating" (Ryan & von Alphen 1993: 110) specifically and implicitly excludes story, because the story is in mind, and the narrative, its representation and systematics are exclusively elements of the information stream. Narratology is definitively about information, not knowledge. Narrative, not story. Text structure, not meaning. A narratology that excludes the story is surely nonsensical, because story is *meaningful* narrative. To make Professor Pavel happy again, and to make narratology a cohesive and entire discipline that includes the heart and head as well as the skeleton, I argue that narratology must recognise that its domain runs the full length of the communication between an author and a receiver and embraces the processes of both and the dynamic between them. The use of a constructivist approach is intended to facilitate narratology in embracing story as well as narrative, and thereby include meaning and thereby become meanin*gful* as a discipline.

1.3.1 The Readerly and the Writerly

To finish up this section, let us use more of Barthes' work for another two useful terms: the readerly and the writerly. There are several states of a story in its lifecycle. A story begins in the mind of a writer as the vision and ideas that they wish to communicate. The writer telescopes this, through the limiting medium of language, into a **text** that represents their vision and messages as best as they can, given those limitations. This text is then passed on to the readers, and that is all they have. The author plays no further part. The text is left to fight alone on behalf of the author's vision and message. Barthes describes this as the "pitiless divorce" between a writer and his readers (Barthes, 1990, p.4); a "destruction of the author" which he completes in his article, *The Death of the Author* (Barthes, 1968). Lovely.

But the text alone *cannot* represent the author. The text is a lifeless, dormant object. It's just a huge signifier, and like any other signifier, it doesn't mean anything by itself. It's a pile of paper with symbols blotched on it, until the symbol language is interpreted by a human being with sufficient mental capability and language skills (what Barthes called 'competence' in reading) to transmute the text into meaning in mind. The reader needs adequate foundational knowledge into which he can connect the new knowledge contained in the text. A two-year-old does not have the language skills or cultural understanding to accurately absorb Shakespeare. A non-Greek speaker cannot enjoy a text in which the symbols are Greek.

Reading is an active role for a reader — completely independent of the author, of course — an individual act of interpretation and an exercise in reading competence. At the basic level, where signifiers are converted into their denoted signifieds, this is a 'readerly' act. If the text says: 'The cat sat on the mat' there is very little interpretive work required of the reader. At this level, interpretation still takes place, but once the sign has been composed (that is, an appropriate signified is created in mind from the basic signifier — 'cat', 'mat' and the causal logic involving them) the gap is filled and the sign is denoted. Very little imagination is required of the reader to create in mind a story that accurately represents the author's vision and intent. Interpretation at this entry level is called 'readerly work'. An author can rely upon a 'competent reader' to denote the correct meaning in mind.

When the text is not denoted, where significations and narrafications abound and need to be connotated into meaning made from the reader's own cultural knowledge and experience, this is what Barthes calls a 'writerly' act. The receiver of the information is doing work in producing a complete narrative in mind from the minimal information they are given. This production in mind — a dual production between the denoted text provided by the author (the readerly) and the knowledge added by the production work of the receiver (the writerly) is the full story.

A Writerly Example

As an example of this, let's read a novel together. This 'novel' was purportedly written by Ernest Hemingway although its origins cannot be substantiated (see, Miller, 1991, p.27). It comprises six words which are, taken together, believed to represent the shortest novel ever written:

FOR SALE. BABY'S SHOES. NEVER WORN.

Before you continue reading, just stop and think a little about the work you do in mind in interpreting these six words into what makes logical sense to you.

It is possible to simply read this text in a literal, readerly manner, and intuit a narrafication comprising a classified advertisement in a publication, in which a person is selling a pair of shoes. However, the 'competent' reader does more. Indeed, the competent reader is helpless, because significations and narrafications drive the unconscious mind to do the writerly work. Driven by cultural knowledge and experience, imagination is projected into the gaps in causal logic left by the author, and a story emerges in mind. The reader converts the denoted text into a narrative which comprises concepts that exist only in mind and which are present only because of the receiver's cultural knowledge and experience. This is 'writerly' work, creating a production of the story through interpretation, and built entirely in the mind of the receiver, using their personal experience to draw the author's vision and messages out of themselves. This is the key to the craft of story creation. The deployment of denoted material crafted to force a receiver into writerly work. A story is dimensionally greater than the sum of the parts because of the work done and the contribution made by the receiver, and it is part of the writer's craft to create the conditions under which these leaps from denotation (readerly) to connotation (writerly) take place.

In creating a story, the competent reader does a proportion of the work in producing the story for themselves. They take ownership of production. And because this writerly production is unique to the individual receiver's knowledge and experience, every reading of a story is a unique production in mind. The skill of the author is to frame the information in such a way as to coax most receivers to project into the same gaps in similar ways and thereby create and enjoy the same story, albeit in each receiver's own, personalised way through the writerly work they did to complete it.

Reception Theory

In academic terms, specifying the mindset of the audience is a dangerous game to play. It is part of a discipline known as reception theory, and I do not intend to cross a line into that arena. It is unwise to attempt to specify the mindset of an audience, either individually or as a corporate conscience, so although I have described some conditions here which appear to cross that line, you will note that I did not go so far as to describe what story the receiver may have created. It can be assumed that recipients of the Hemingway shortest novel will have interpreted a (writerly) story into mind that is abstracted from the (readerly) content of the classified advertisement; however, I did not specify what the writerly story is, I merely note that writerly work takes place. In narratological terms, it is my intention to go this far and no further. To identify the triggers that cause writerly work, but not to attempt to specify the content or nature or results of that writerly work.

The conundrum is that narratologists are being commendably sensible when they avoid the treacherous waters of psychology. Let us leave that to the psychologists; we narratologists are involved with story and the Arts. My research therefore attempts to broaden narratology only enough to embrace the components of mental process that triggers the writerly work, and no further. For this to be acceptable as a boundary to my research, we must understand a little about how consciousness and memory function.

1.4   Narrative and Consciousness

When we think of the *self*, we identify a body and a mind. The body is quantified as the physical manifestation of the self, but what is a mind? We see the brain as part of the body, a physical component, in which the mind is somehow contained, and the mind is doing the mystical, almost magical, feeling, knowing and experiencing. We see the brain as material and the mind as the thoughts, emotions, spirit and soul that gives us an ethereal presence we call consciousness.

Contemporary thinking asserts a somewhat different model. Antonio Damasio (2010) maps out how consciousness has evolved on the physical side from pre-historic brain stem through cumulative layers of developing brain, each associated with stages of evolution. He addresses the mental/physical relationship from basic responses to stimuli (for example, the way a woodlouse curls up into a ball when facing danger) through an ability to act and to react purposefully to external events (such as birds using tools; rats solving puzzles) on up to high-functioning subjectivity and insightful knowledge of self, with the ability to remember past events and project forwards to an imagined future. In human terms, Damasio characterises these 'levels' of consciousness as the "protoself" with primordial feelings; the "core self" an action-driven protagonist reacting and interacting in the world; and the "autobiographical self", which incorporates self-knowledge, mental time-travel, social and spiritual dimensions (Damasio, 2010).

You may not feel you have much in common with a woodlouse, however, human brain development has evolved through many phases across millennia of evolution and the protoself level of brain function is still there within us. When we carry out sophisticated mental tasks, we still need all the layers of brain operation to contribute to the whole. Although neuroscience tends to separate the brain into functional units, this is for logical reasons. Brain function cannot be entirely viewed as modular operational units or obsolete areas that no longer serve any purpose. They all work together to create one consciousness. This section then, with acknowledgement to Damasio, provides an overview of the levels of development that comprise consciousness, demonstrating a through-line to how narrative becomes part of a contemporary understanding of human consciousness.

1.4.1 The Protoself

The protoself is, according to Damasio (2010), an integrated collection of separate neural patterns that map, moment by moment, the most stable aspects of the organism's physical structure. Protoself maps are distinctive in that they generate not merely body images but also felt body images. These primordial feelings of the body are spontaneously present in the normal awake brain. Primordial feeling are the baseline feelings of *being* that the protoself, in its native state, spontaneously and relentlessly delivers, instant upon instant. The protoself is about establishing and maintaining homeostasis in the context of the world in which the organism is situated. The protoself level is about existence and self: it...

> "[...] corresponds to a gathering of information regarding the state of the body. It is constructed in the brain stem and it generates feelings that signify our existence" (Damasio, 2011).

1.4.2 The Core Self

Our woodlouse is reactive to stimuli from changes in the world. Although consciousness is dependent upon responses to objects in the world, the core self developed initially through reactionary, and later controlled, relationships with those objects, along with the feelings that are generated by interaction and association with an object. Damasio calls the core self the "protagonist [in] this wordless narrative as an account of what is transpiring, in life as well as in the brain, but not yet as an interpretation." (Damasio, 2010, p.201, 204). The core self is an ongoing description of events concerning the 'protagonist'; an organism which is now recognising events rather than simply existing in a 'now' but is not yet self-aware within that context. The core self is about a proactive presence and identity.

1.4.3 The Autobiographical Self

According to Damasio, the evolution of an autobiographical self brought elaborate coordinating mechanisms whereby past memories can be retrieved and treated as singular here-and-now objects in the mapping and imaging processes of the core self. The core self reacts to (and triggers) momentary changes, such as a change in adrenalin or dopamine levels in the body, however the autobiographical self can also bring memories and projected scenarios to bear as mental object that can impact response.

> "The autobiographical self creates the more or less coherent picture of our history, a narrative with a lived past and an anticipated future. The narrative is culled from real events, from imaginary events, and from past interpretations and re-interpretations of events" (Damasio, 2011).

Memories and projections are narratives, however they are treated as objects in mind, and incorporated into thinking, just like any other objects used in cognitive mapping. By melding a sense of past and future objects with moment-by-moment objects, a meta-object can be envisaged as an event. Thus we can think of 'World War II' as a single 'unit' of memory even though in reality it is a long and complex narrative.

In this way, a narrative context at the heart of a definition for 'self' becomes evident. Indeed, it is fundamental. The world spins and creates change over time. The sun rises and sets, it warms and cools, the tide goes out and comes in, light becomes dark becomes light and the first cells show the first inklings of life through the basic energy transfer inherent in these cyclic patterns. As creatures of the earth, we are *functions of* the natural cycles which spawn and energise life and define our being and the nature of self. Everything is a narrative consequence.

Thus, our senses are a function of the narrative context in which we live. "There can be no consciousness without feelings" (Damasio, 2010, p.242) and this remains true irrespective of our sophistication. What are feelings? They are a mental appreciation of a 'now' defined by situating the self in this ever-changing narrative context. Our nerve endings and our sense of touch are integral parts of our minds; the parts of our mind that sense the world; a world that is not as a single, static object, but the very definition of change over time. Change over time — the basis of life. The world is not a static object, it is 'life', and consciousness is not a brain; it is an integrated holistic knowing of the world and our (ever-changing) situation within it. If there was no change over time on earth, we would not exist. Each person is a manifest narrative born out of (and contributing to) a world that is a narrative. Existence has human meaning because it is narrative.

Our mindset at any given moment is a melded combination of being in the now (protoself homeostasis plus core sensory monitoring) but with added 'objects' that include events and autobiographical knowledge from the past and a projected future which give a narrative context (that is, they include 'protagonistic' experience) to our core self.

As a consequence, every part of our being is a part of our consciousness. Not simply the mind in the brain but the perceptions of the five senses, the signals from somatic organs, the emotional responses, the feeling in your tummy and the pain in your tooth, the heat of guilt from what you did yesterday, the anxiety concerning tomorrow's challenge, the way you feel about the look on that face — it is all part of your consciousness; the *knower* that is you and the knower that *feels*. The mind is a myriad of feeling-inspired images and maps, emotions and reactions, pulled together into a centre that manages causal logic; a causal logic that is a function of the world and our place in it. It takes all this information from all these sources, and it processes and crunches this data continuously and organises it into narrative understanding.

> In interplay with the brain stem and thalamus, the cortex constructs the maps that become mind. In interplay with the brain stem and thalamus, the cortex helps generate the core self. Last, using the records of past activity stored in its vast memory banks, the cerebral cortex constructs our biography, replete with the experience of the physical and social environments we have inhabited. The cortex provides us with an identity and places us at the center of the wondrous, forward-moving spectacle that is our conscious mind (Damasio, 2010, pp. 248-249).

Having evolved a high-functioning autobiographical self, with a sense of knowing, of insight into self, of subjectivity and imagination, the outcome is the ongoing, continuous narrative that is your life, unfolding within (and contributing to) the narrative that is continuous change over time on Earth. Add to this the autobiographical self that comes with self-awareness and these narratives can be interpreted into human meaning in mind, made knowable through mental time-travel; that is, narrative memory and speculative projection for how a narrative can be predicted and manipulated.

We are born out of nature's narratives, so once sophisticated communication came along, it was only natural that narrative would be at the core of our method for sharing knowledge. Our extraordinary ability to communicate through language has rendered narration also the syntactic unit of shared knowledge.

1.4.4 Consciousness and Stories

How can we use this contemporary understanding of neuroscience to illuminate the power of stories? How can we apply it to everyday people and behaviours? In this section I will present the functions of mind in two situations: firstly, depicting a mind experiencing a life event and secondly, a mind receiving a narration. The similarities between the two reveal the visceral processes that are triggered and used by stories and are therefore applicable to a constructivist narratology.

Figure 3: You in Motion is a (simplified) representation of the first two mental dynamics at play in normal, everyday circumstances: core consciousness and autobiographical narrative memories.

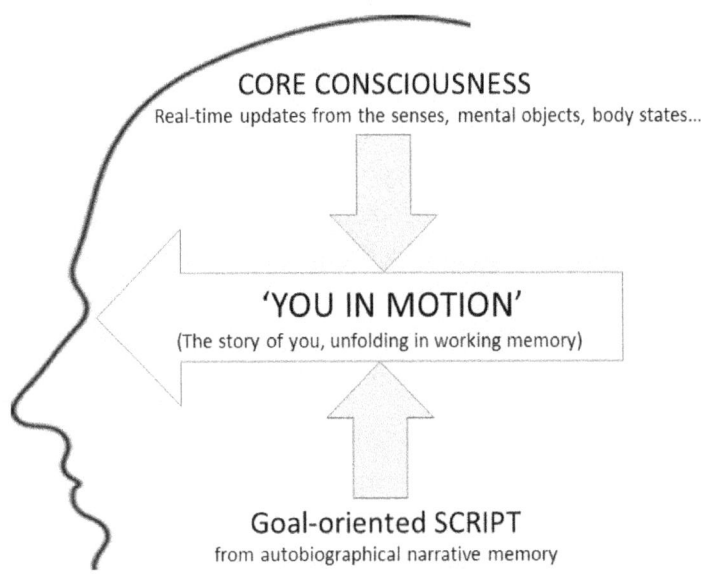

Figure 3: You in Motion

The large arrows in the diagram represent the basic functions of a mind in what I call an idling state; that is, awake, but performing a familiar activity that does not make high demands on the higher cognitive functions. This state represents any regular routine, such as making tea, catching a train, making a purchase in a shop or eating in a restaurant. Anything familiar that the owner of this mind has done before, such that it is retained in long term memory as a 'script' that can be re-run whenever the predictable outcome of that routine is desired.

The template for performing such a task — known in neuroscience as a schema or script — is drawn from long-term, autobiographical narrative memory and placed as an 'object' into working memory where it is used to guide the owner from the current state, step by step, to the desired outcome. As the script runs, the owner's core consciousness delivers moment-by-moment real-world status updates into working memory. This real-world status is compared to the desired situation prescribed by the script. Where there are differences between the two, real-world adjustments are made to keep the organism on track to achieve the beneficial outcome of running the script.

At any point in a human life, many scripts may be active; some short (wash, get breakfast, walk to work, do some shopping, make tea, put one foot in front of the other...) some of medium duration (make a train journey, attend a lecture, have a holiday); and some long (a career path, a relationship, parenting). Indeed, multiple scripts run simultaneously, however, let us focus on just the one. This continuous comparison of the organism's position in the script against the situation in the real world, and the adjustments made as a result, creates what I have termed You in Motion: the continuous unfolding of the organism in the real world as a confluence of the intent implicit to the scripts and the actuality reported by core consciousness. You in motion is the story of you.

For example, if making a train journey, the 'catching a train' script provides the steps to follow to achieve the goal — arrival at a desired destination. As you set about the tasks, the embodied responses and the senses guide you to ensure this particular instance of the script is successful. For example, the walk to the station will be essentially the same every time but will be unique in some ways that must be managed. One must avoid bumping into other people, buy the right ticket for this particular journey, find the right platform, find a vacant seat, leave the train at the right station and so forth. The 'you in motion' is a result of working memory continuously comparing the requirement of the script against the real-time situation, refining your status in the world to stay on track until the desired outcome is achieved.

It is important to note that working with scripts in this way is not intellectually onerous. While the requirements of the script and the actuality in the real world are similar, you make few demands on your higher cognitive functions. Your 537th train commute to work is unlikely to be memorable in any way and may not require any exceptional active mental effort. As Roger Schank tells us:

> Scripts replace thinking. The thinking people do is to decide which script to apply. (Schank, 1991, p.49)

Running scripts becomes so unconscious that we can achieve the ends largely on 'auto-pilot'. This is how, after spending years of concentrated effort learning to walk, we ultimately come to do it without thinking about it. We learn through repetition until the script can do the job for us and leave our higher functions largely free to think about other things.

However, what happens when we do not have a script we can apply to a situation or when the script that is running is no longer fit for purpose? What if something goes wrong such that simply continuing to step through the script will not automatically get us to the desired outcome?

The failure of the script becomes evident to the organism through a divergence between the reporting from core consciousness and what the script prescribes, as depicted in **Figure 4**, below.

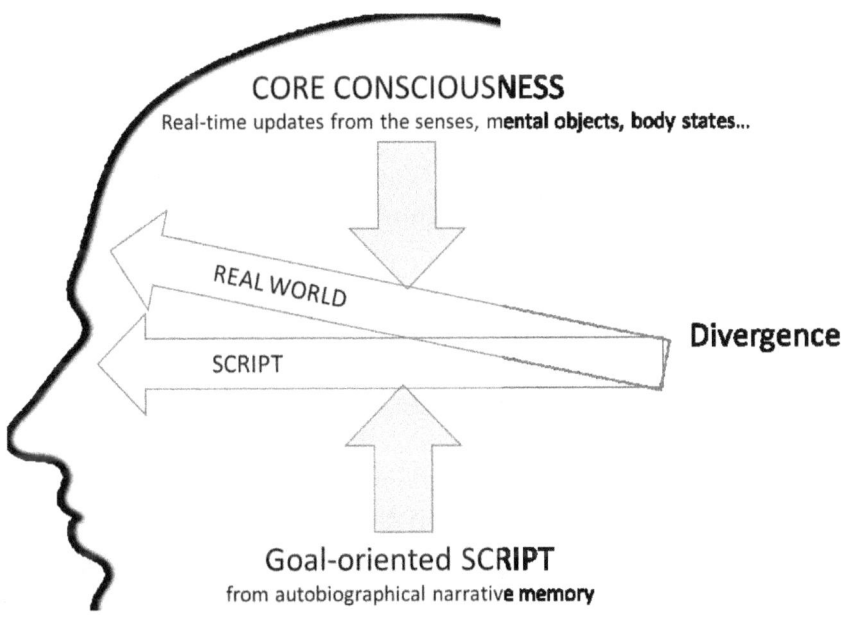

Figure 4: Divergence between the script and real-world events

Up until now, running the script has been relatively mindless. However, a gap of this nature, between the requirement of the script and the reality in the world is sensed in working memory and acts as a trigger for the owner to apply active intelligence to the situation. The **higher cognitive functions** are brought to bear on the situation, as depicted by the thin arrows in **Figure 5**.

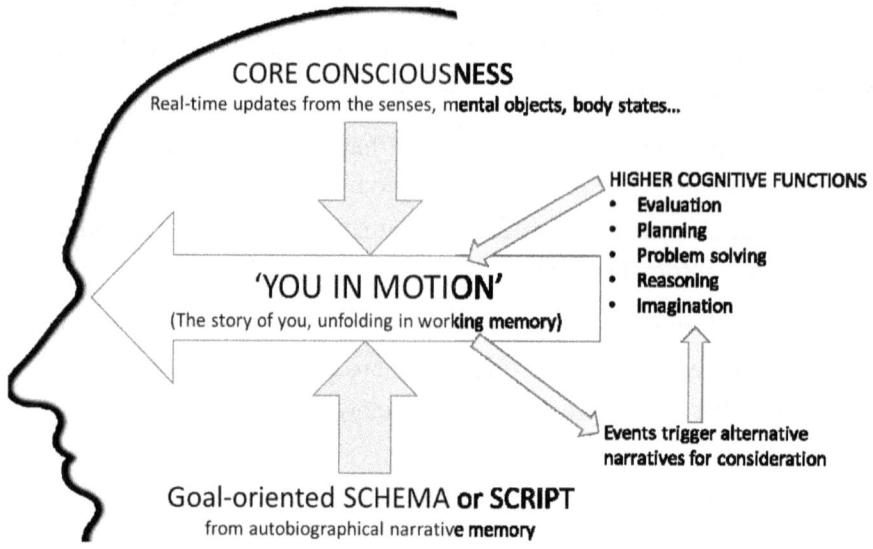

Figure 5: The Higher Cognitive Functions

The higher cognitive functions address the divergence between the script and the real world through capacities such as reasoning and imagination in a combination of three ways:

1. Through manipulating the world to close that gap and bring the existing script back on to the right path. For example, a blocked path on the walk to the railway station could be fixed through an alternative route.
2. Through establishing a new or alternative narrative progression (script) that will achieve the desired ends. For example, if the train is cancelled, the script is no longer fit for purpose, and the owner might choose to get her and drive the journey instead.
3. Through giving up on the aims of the failing script; setting new aims and an alternative path. For example, taking the day off and writing a book instead. (That's what I would do.)

I argue that one major facet of intelligence is the ability to react to narrative disruption in these ways. We feel mentally aroused when we cannot see the path that a narrative needs to take for us to remain in balance as a human being relying upon such scripts. In evolutionary terms, a gap in a narrative of this nature is a instinctual indicator of danger, risk or opportunity. The protoself responds to narrative disruption, with physical and somatic changes that raise the warning levels. As Ernst Gombrich argues:

> Our whole sensory apparatus is basically tuned to the monitoring of unexpected change. Continuity fails to register after a time, and this is true both on the physiological and the psychological level. (Gombrich, 1994, p.108)

The script is no longer fit for purpose, so the higher cognitive functions are triggered to find new solutions. Intelligence is the ability to rebuild or contrive a new narrative path to a beneficial outcome; to use and/or combine scripts, to project reasoning and imagination into the gaps in the creation of an effective script in the mind that will achieve the desired aims in the face of this narrative disruption. I argue that the responses to these gaps contribute strongly to the success of the organism. The creation of an effective narrative is a fundamental requirement for survival.

> " 'Intelligence' is the ability to attain goals in the face of obstacles by means of decisions and actions based on rational rules. The quality 'intelligence' is awarded to those who follow story structure" (Pinker, 2007).

Let us assume that we are eating in a restaurant. We have done it many times before, so the *eating in a restaurant* script is applied and we are stepping through the process. Make a reservation, travel to the restaurant, meet the *maître d'*, find the table, use the menus to secure food, taste the wine, engage in stimulating conversation, argue over the bill, process payments and so on. We have done it before, so the shared script runs in the background leaving us to focus our minds on the stimulating conversation. However, what happens if there is a disruption to the script? Let's say one of our neighbouring diners begins to choke. They stand up, grasp their throat, choking. Then fall, dying, to the floor.

Our script is now divergent from actual events. Gaps are evident between the cognitive map derived from core consciousness (the representation of the real world) and the prescribed steps of the script, and these gaps trigger the higher cognitive functions to search for new narrative logic that will fill or bridge this gap and return the organism's world to balance: Is there a doctor present? No. Call an ambulance? No time. A sharp whack in the small of the back? Nothing is working. Time is ticking away. Then, one of the party lifts the person up, gets behind them and applies the Heimlich manoeuvre. On the third pelvic thrust, the obstruction is expelled, and the victim is saved.

Those who witnessed the event and have never seen the Heimlich manoeuvre before now have a new narrative in their minds. The narrative disruption was filled by the Heimlich manoeuvre, creating a new (to them) narrative in the witnesses' working memory; a series of steps that served a valuable purpose. That new narrative makes sense and — most importantly — is a complete, logical narrative which achieves a clear outcome, and these are the conditions for it to be lain down in autobiographical narrative memory. This is the mental process involved in learning through life experience. The retention of the process as a memory is an automatic, unconscious action triggered by the recognition of a complete narrative, creating a memory that could be offered up as a possible solution in the future when a person is choking. Repeated deployment or experience of a narrative consolidates the script in long-term memory and renders it more likely to be offered by the unconscious mind in future when aspects of reality pattern-match against elements of a narrative script.

Note just how many of the terms I have used in describing consciousness and mental functions are related to story. Script, protagonist, narrative, goals, motivation, outcomes. This is because stories are a function of these mechanisms of mind.

Mental modes and story

Now let's flip the stimulus and investigate what happens if the experience being processed is not a life event, but a fictional narration.

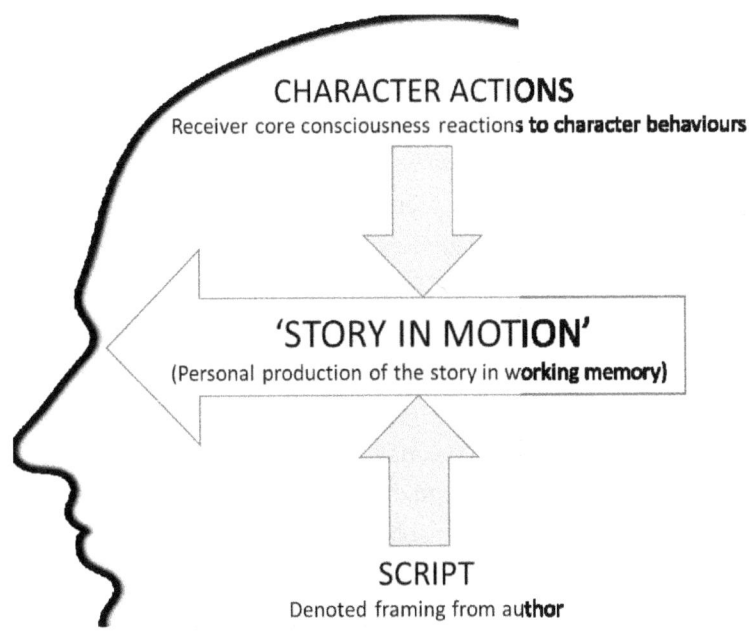

Figure 6: Story in Motion

Notice the subtle differences in what is now going on. The mind is behaving in a similar way, using the same mechanisms and dynamics, but the *sources of information* that stimulate the 'story in motion' are different. In particular, the script is triggered through the denoted information delivered by the author, and the continuous monitoring of progress by the senses does not monitor the real world, but the actions and reactions of the characters and the changes in the situation in the story world.

Let's say the author gives the audience a scenario where a character simply must have a successful restaurant meal with a client if she is to secure a major deal. This framing raises the question in the mind of the receiver of the story: Will the meeting in the restaurant go smoothly? Will she land the big deal? And the receiver loads up a *business meeting in a restaurant* script in their working memory similar to the one they might load if they were the protagonist in the restaurant in real life.

Now, as the receiver looks over the shoulder of the protagonist, instead of the receiver's core consciousness monitoring the real-world and reacting to keep the script on track, the characters in the story act as a proxy. It is the characters who react to the situation, and it is their reactions that the receiver of the story can evaluate in working memory in the context of the loaded script. The receiver's embodied responses and perception of the situation are still delivering into working memory as they do in a real-world experience; however, in a narration, they must accommodate the ongoing actions taken by the characters rather than changes in the world through the receiver's own actions. The receiver organises the 'story in motion' in working memory, creating a narrative that draws not only on the script and the character actions, but also on the context the receiver provides for themselves in terms of presumptions about past events and speculations regarding what is to come, both of which must also be reconfigured continuously as events unfold in ways that were not accurately predicted. This means, of course, that the sum of what the author gives us (to inspire a script into working memory) plus what the characters do (to drive the core consciousness responses into working memory) rarely amounts to a settled picture for the receiver of the narration. There are gaps between expectation and what happens, and because the receiver is never in control of the unfolding narrative, the receiver is relentlessly exercised in attempting to build a story that fills every gap and makes satisfying sense. It is the author who is, to a greater extent, in control of the story in motion.

Let us assume that the author sets up the protagonist's mission to make it through the restaurant meal with her businessman and win her big deal... but he starts to choke. At this point, there are differences between the expectation set by the author and the possibility of achieving the aim of the narrative (there is no deal if he chokes to death). We now have the situation represented in **Figure 7: Divergence through narration**.

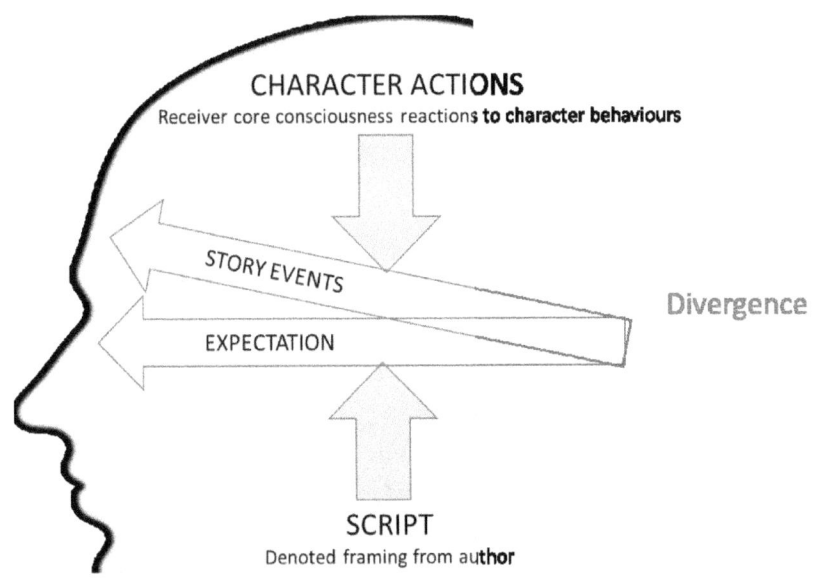

Figure 7: Divergence through narration

Even though the script was inspired into mind by the author, and the progress of the script towards the beneficial outcome was driven by the character actions, the divergence between expectation and what happens works in the same way as a real world experience and triggers the *receiver's* instinctive response: to project intelligence into the gaps to find a solution to the problem, like this:

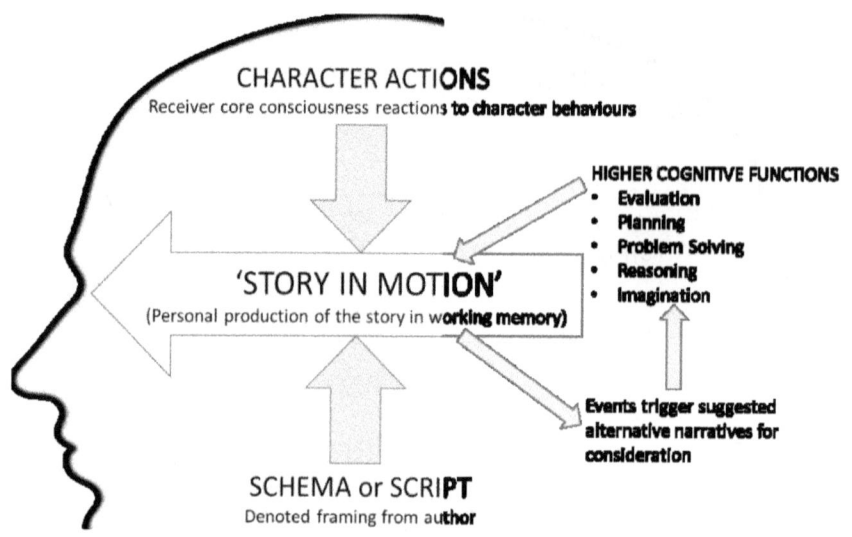

Figure 8: Knowledge Gaps in Narration

As in the real-world scenario, the gaps in the cognitive map in working memory trigger a response from the higher cognitive functions. Even though we are absorbing a narration, as receivers, we do not passively wait to see what happens, we project into the gaps as if it is happening to us. As Bordwell suggests:

> In the course of constructing the story, the perceiver uses schemata [scripts] and incoming cues to make assumptions, draw inferences about current story events, and frame and test hypotheses about prior and upcoming events (Bordwell, 1985, p.35).

Notice how the information sources are no longer life events, they are narrated events, but when the gaps are opened between the script expectation and actuality, the 'story in motion' that is built in mind is completed *in the same way as for the real-world event*; that is, through the receiver's instinctive drive to activate their own imagination and reasoning, plus alternative scripts and possibilities suggested from long-term memory, and project them into the gaps. These projected possibilities are not from the author or the characters. They are drawn from the receiver's higher cognitive functions and autobiographical narrative memory. They are triggered by the author crafting gaps into the denoted framework and by character actions, thereby raising questions in the mind of the receiver concerned with what will happen next and causing the receiver to project possible solutions — from their own history and experience — into the gaps in knowledge.

Let us continue with the story. What does happen next? The desired narrative progression is disrupted by the man's choking. The chances of a successful outcome to the meeting are low. Then, the protagonist administers the Heimlich manoeuvre, and saves the businessman's life. He recovers and is grateful. They bond over the life-saving events of what was supposed to be a lunch, and the deal is sealed.

If the receiver of the narration has never experienced the Heimlich manoeuvre before, they build a new (to them) story in mind and learn a new narrative solution (the Heimlich manoeuvre) to a life problem (a person choking). A complete narrative which makes sense, so it is lain down in long-term autobiographical memory using the same mental mechanisms as for a real life experience.

Indeed, given this particular example, there is evidence that this has happened many times. People with no medical training have experienced the Heimlich manoeuvre in a narration and, when later faced with a choking individual in the real world, have found that they know the Heimlich manoeuvre, have administered it successfully in the real world and saved a person's life. This is the power of knowledge gaps in a narrative driving a memory into the mind of the receiver. Saviours have included children who have watched, for example *Spongebob Squarepants*:

http://time.com/4103402/teen-who-saved-choking-classmate-says-spongebob-taught-him-heimlich-maneuver/

And Disney's *A.N.T. Farm:*

http://abcnews.go.com/blogs/headlines/2012/05/6-year-old-saves-best-friends-life-with-heimlich-maneuver/

And this one – a seven-year-old girl saves her mother having seen the film *Mrs Doubtfire* (1993, director Chris Columbus):

http://newsfeed.time.com/2013/11/18/mrs-doubtfire-is-not-only-the-most-brilliant-film-of-our-time-it-also-saved-a-womans-life/

These links may not work at the time you read this, however, an internet search will return you many examples of individuals who have experienced the Heimlich manoeuvre in story and gone on to apply it in their lives. A memory laid down through absorbing a story. A memory that saves a life.

Note that in each of these cases, the saviour had not been taught or even tried to learn the Heimlich manoeuvre. They were relaxing; watching the television in their down-time when the memory was made. But made it was. The sedentary act of absorbing a story caused a memory to be created that later saved a life.

The reason this is of interest is because it demonstrates how a story can be used to stimulate visceral mental reflexes and affect a receiver's actual knowledge and unconscious responses. In experiencing a narration, the *information* sources are no longer life events, they are narrated events, but when the narrative expectation is disrupted gaps are opened within the narrative logic building in the receiver's working memory and the *knowledge* that goes into the gaps comes from the same place; namely, the receiver's personal intellect, driven by their own cultural knowledge, history and experience.

The first two essential elements are denoted within the narration: a framework from the author and the actions and behaviours of the characters. However, because they add up to a narrafication with gaps in it, *the same instinctive responses are triggered* in the receiver of the story as they are in life. The higher cognitive functions are brought to bear and begin to project into the gaps in order to create a complete *story* in mind that has meaning and makes causal logic sense. When the receiver uses their intellect and personal knowledge and experience to complete the story in this way, this is what I have called **the storification of the sign**.

Autobiographical Narrative Memory

This is my own term, drawn largely from the work of Damasio, and developed in my contribution to *Narrative and Metaphor in Education* (Hanne and Kaal (Eds.), 2018). I argue that this type of memory is the common denominator between life experience and fictional narration. In a fictional narration, if it is created with knowledge gaps, the mental processes of the receiver deploy in the same way as they do for a real-world experience. That is why stories are so important. A person can learn something new through direct experience and they can learn something new through absorbing a story *provided* it is crafted with knowledge gaps that trigger the same mental processes that lay down a memory. The narrative created and built in mind through filling these gaps is called a story, the process of building this story in this way is storification. That is, a joint effort between the author delivering a scenario with gaps in the knowledge required, and the receiver filling these gaps with knowledge from their own history and experience. The resulting narrative in mind, if it makes sense in human causal logic terms, becomes a memory.

Both life narratives and fictional narratives can trigger the storification response. In the latter case, it is the author crafting knowledge gaps into the narrative that trigger the story to be produced in the mind, and because it has narrative logic and consequences, and uses the same mental dynamics as a life experience, the receiver still lays it down as an autobiographical narrative memory.

I argue that this is what makes storytelling different from other forms of communication. The gaps in knowledge force writerly work to be done in the mind of the person receiving a narration, and this work must be done for the story to make sense. By doing this work, the receiver tailors the final 'production' in mind to their own mindset and completes the narrative logic to their unique personal specification. That is why I maintain that narratology is misguided when it looks for the substance of a story in the structure of an existing text. The resonance of a narration with a human mind comes from the writerly work done in the mind of a person receiving a narration. The gaps trigger the receiver into contributing to the content of the story; producing it for themselves by projecting knowledge from their own history, experience and intellect into the gaps crafted into place by an author. It is the knowledge that is missing from the meaning in the text that causes resonance and instinctive engagement.

This is why it is very difficult to remember 20 items on a tray, and yet essentially effortless to remember an entire story you were told when you were four years old. (Could you recount *Little Red Riding Hood* right now? *The*

Three Little Pigs? The Hare and the Tortoise? The Ugly Duckling?) The 20 items do not comprise a narrative (although this is why the experts tell you to make up a story from the 20 items in order to remember them). The 20 items do not work with your brain. Your brain prefers a narrative in order to make sense and remember. A story, on the other hand, is memory shaped. You never *tried* to memorise *Little Red Riding Hood* and those children who saved lives did not *try* to learn the Heimlich manoeuvre. The narrative form simply locks into memory through unconscious processes and your mind cannot help but remember. A story is a shareable version of a memory that fits the way your mind wants material arranged.

The story begins in the mind of the author and, through the joint effort involved in the communication between the author and the receiver, it ends up in the mind of the receiver. In focussing on the inherent structures in a text, narratology is not concerning itself with the story *at all*. That is why narratology has weaknesses that render it less useful than it should be to those who work with **story** and those who look to narratology to explain **story**. Narratology does not address story communication. It addresses narrative communication. Narratology addresses information; story is concerned with knowledge. Narratology addresses denotation; story is concerned with connotation. Narratology addresses media and narrative communication; story addresses mind and meaning. In each of these pairs, narratology needs to address both.

From this perspective, the syntactic and semantic unit of thought, memory, story and linguistics is narrative. That is how fundamental narrative is, and how enormous the opportunity is for narratology to centre itself at the core of human function.

1.4.5 Knowledge and Gaps

You may have noticed that knowledge gaps have been mentioned with an increasing degree of regularity. In the processes of mind under discussion knowledge gaps are the triggers that demand the writerly work that populates the gap with knowledge from the receiver's own cultural experience and transforms the event (in life or in narration) into a unique story in mind. To demonstrate just how fundamental knowledge gaps are in driving our deepest, most innate protoself responses I would like to take you through a fascinating example, drawn from Steven Pinker's book, *How the Mind Works* (Pinker, 1999).

The Impossible Problem

Pinker asks us to consider how the human eye and a high-definition camera do the same job. Both very effectively project a comprehensive high-definition image. However, whilst the computer scientists congratulate themselves on the image they have generated, this is not the final product. For the brain, the retinal image is the raw input, from which it must make sense of the information and derive meaning. This presents a problem to software engineering, because although it is relatively easy to imitate the eye and generate an image, it is extremely difficult to derive meaning from what it sees. Indeed, so difficult has this problem (known as 'inverse optics') proven to be that, according to Pinker, it cannot be done.

> Just as it is easy to multiply two numbers and announce the product, but impossible to take a product and announce the numbers that were multiplied to get it, so optics is easy, but inverse optics is impossible (Pinker, 1999, p.28).

And yet the brain solves this supposedly impossible problem every time we open our eyes. How does it manage that? The answer is that the mind supplies the missing information. A brain can only make sense of an image comprising an aggregation of edges, textures, shades, light and colours if it makes assumptions, projects into gaps, speculates on expectation — and then relies upon this greater quantity of information it contributes to the overall picture for itself in order to make decisions. It achieves this by drawing on conditioning and instinct, personal experience, information from all the senses, and millennia of evolution. According to Pinker, this is why optical illusions work — they play on our natural drive to create human sense from whatever information is given. A television is nothing but a grouping of rapidly-changing coloured lights, but our brain pattern-matches the visual stimuli against knowledge and experience, just as it does in the real world, fills in the missing information and perceives a world that makes human sense behind the screen. We cannot help but do this because our brains instinctively pattern-match and instinctively rush to fill in the missing information.

I argue that there are two more assumptions that we make to complete the picture. Firstly, the image triggers a phenomenological framework in mind; a context of other signs and significations that give contextual sense to this one, as we did earlier with the flower inspiring a different framing mindset for each context (birthday celebration, funeral, romance…). Secondly, the picture is situated sequentially into a narrafication — the picture is pattern-matched against the context of the narrative logic of the most applicable script known to the receiver that includes this image. In this way, the dimension of change over time that delivers the cause/effect chain is built around the image and therefore makes sense in a narrative context.

This is just the eye, and just the retinal image. This 'impossible' problem is surely solved continuously in relation to all the senses, motor and somatic functions of human activity throughout the moment-by-moment creation of a perpetual You in Motion. As we live our lives largely by running any number of concurrent active scripts, so we understand any snapshot in the context of what probably goes before it in the most applicable narrative and what experience tells us is likely to come next. If you see an action shot of a tennis player in a newspaper, you contextualise this in mind as both a person (signifier) and a tennis player (signification), you situate them into a context with racquets and balls and another player hitting the balls back and forth (narrafication) and from there into a cultural basis, with the rules of tennis, the injustices and controversies, the personalities and fortunes of individual players, the tension and excitement of the game, the reasons they are in a thing called a 'newspaper', and so on (storification).

All this from a single image, and yet this is standard behaviour. I argue that much of human physical and psychological makeup follows this model, whereby the challenge to the brain is to solve an inverse (and 'impossible'!) problem of this nature. Human beings receive information to the senses but must convert that information into knowledge. That transformation includes assumptions which are primarily drawn from personal experience and therefore the likelihood that the information that pattern-matches against a moment in a narrative script will be correct. The tennis player action-shot is unlikely to have been taken in a context of, say, a battlefield or at the top of Mount Everest or in a political anti-chamber. The context we load for a tennis player is generally the same for all of us who have grown up in the western world. Most of our lives are lived within these known, predictable, reliable contexts. Every moment is a well understood snapshot of ourselves on the path of one of many well understood and predictable scripts. This is essential for us to manage a controlled, non-chaotic life.

We desire knowledge because human evolution has favoured the best problem solvers. Natural selection has refined us: the best mind is the best problem solver. The best problem solver is the mind best able to project knowledge into gaps. The best arrangement of knowledge is that which creates a reliable narrative.

> Each of our mental modules solves its unsolvable problems by making a leap of faith about how the world works, by making assumptions that are indispensable but indefensible — the only defense being that the assumptions worked well enough in the world of our ancestors. (Pinker, 1999, p.30)

It seems, then, that we are dependent upon the scripts we hold in autobiographical narrative memory for understanding our context moment by moment and using the narrative we build in getting through life. An interesting way to view this hypothesis is to rationalise it from the other perspective: relying solely upon your cognition and intellect without any scripts to apply will not get your through the day. A situation without a script is a version of 'the impossible problem'.

> Sensory stimuli alone cannot determine a percept, since they are incomplete and ambiguous. The organism constructs a perceptual judgment on the basis of nonconscious inferences. (Bordwell, 1985b, p.31)

Without a narrative script from our knowledge and experience to apply, we are lost. A baby is born with no narratives, and is helpless. Sensory stimuli leave it unknowing because knowledge requires a narrative context. The role of education is to generate and 'memorise' narratives. One measure of intelligence is the ability to select, apply and manipulate narrative scripts in order to obtain the desired outcomes in life.

> Story is the organising principle for human action. Humans always seek to use story structure to impose order and organisation on the flow of experience. (Crossley, 2000)

If you are awoken at 2.38am by a bump in the night, you cannot simply roll over and go back to sleep. Your mind will not let you, because it cannot render a complete narrative from the given information (that is, there are knowledge gaps). Your higher cognitive functions are activated, and you will not be able to settle your mind until that narrative is satisfactorily completed with knowledge you accept as reliable. Knowledge gaps are the source of mental activity that is over and above the standard daily routine. When you fill a knowledge gap you create a story. It is outside the normal, known and familiar narrative, so it is elevated into a story worth telling to others: "Did you hear that crash in the night?! I was terrified! I thought we were being robbed! I was off down the stairs stark naked and swinging my nine iron! I thought we were all going to die!"

When it is established that the noise was just Granny making a cup of tea, the knowledge gap is filled, the emotions settled, and the story can be bedded into autobiographical memory. The next time that same noise wakes our protagonist up in the night, he won't be rushing off down the stairs naked and alarmed. He will roll his eyes and pull the quilt over his ears. It does not arouse him this time because he has no knowledge gaps. It is now a script in memory with no gaps, so Granny doesn't end up wearing a nine iron.

It is important to note just how very important these knowledge gaps are. They are at the root of personal advancement. Once a complete new story is created and can be seen to be effective in achieving a known goal, it gets bedded into autobiographical narrative memory as a new usable script. I argue that this is a fundamental and effective form of *learning*. If it gets used often, it becomes a go-to method of handling a common problem. If a script becomes so commonly used that it is passed on to your children, and to your children's children, in the end the behaviour gets hard-wired into the neural pathways and becomes passed on genetically. I would go as far as to suggest tha, taken to its logical extreme across many generations, this could be how instinctive behaviours evolve.

Which brings us to the final stage of our semiotic journey. We began with **signifiers and signifieds** in the creation of a simple linguistic sign, augmented it with personal cultural knowledge and experience to create **signification** in mind. We then added the diachronic dimension — change over time — to create the **narrafication of the sign**. Now we are once again adding personal knowledge and experience to create a narrative-in-mind that is new to the receiver; a narrative they have not experienced before and yet has human causal logic and is fully formed in mind. This is **storification**.

To be clear, any narrative-in-mind, strictly speaking, is a story. However, in my experience as a researcher in this space, a story becomes increasingly compelling the more work the receiver must do and the more original the story is to the receiver. The 'amount' of story present in the narration is a sliding scale. The more readerly it is, the less story it has; the more writerly it is, the more of a compelling story it becomes. As John le Carré said, ' "The cat sat on the mat" is not a story. "The cat sat on the dog's mat" *is* story.' (Le Carré, 1977). I would caveat that. The latter is a story, because it opens up a gap in our mind between the current situation and what may happen when the dog returns. However, 'the cat sat on the mat' is still a story, because it creates a narrative in mind, but it is weak story, because knowledge gaps are minimal and the receiver has very little writerly work to contribute. The more knowledge gaps there are, the more writerly work the receiver has to do. The more writerly work the receiver has to do, the more compelling the story is perceived to be. Obviously, this assertion is subjective and is more a point of interest than formal research. However, in my experience of researching stories and knowledge gaps, it is apparent that the more knowledge gaps there are in a story, the more highly rated the story becomes.

1.5　The Storification of the Sign

When you read a story you do not remember the words on the page, you remember a mental model of meaning that you build in mind for yourself. You become a 'producer' of the story as you make sense of the information you receive and gradually build this mental model. As you do this, and as you add knowledge from your own experience, the story breaks out of the story world and takes on a unique structure and meaning to you in your mind and in your life. This is the storification of the sign. While the narrafication is the understanding of the meaning and events in the story world, storification is the extension of the story beyond the beginning and end of the narration and into a 'meta-meaning' woven in with the life and consciousness of the receiver. The impact is different for every receiver and cannot be specified. The same narration may have a significant effect on one receiver, changing their mindset, worldview, morality or knowledge going forwards, and yet on another individual may have no storification effect whatsoever. Indeed, many storification effects may be unconscious. We simply do not know and certainly cannot specify what storifications take place for any given narration, we can only say that storification does take place.

Narrafication is 'what happens' in the story world, and it requires writerly work to complete. Storification is how this narrafication manifests as meaning in the mind of the receiver, specifically once combined with knowledge from their own personal mindset. As the storification is a subjective and perhaps ethereal phenomenon (rather like the mind itself) the best way of explaining it is through a number of examples.

1) The most obvious examples are the recognition of the morality in a children's story or the traditional understanding of subtext in a novel. If one reads the story of *Little Red Riding Hood* to a four-year-old, and recognises a moral message that is not stated in the denoted text (nor in the understanding of what happens in terms of the narrafication) then a storification has taken place.

2) If a receiver of a narration receives a metaphoric or allegorical meaning, this is a storification. Reading George Orwell's *Animal Farm* and coming away with an implicit critical evaluation of communism is a storification.

3) If you are scared to go in the sea following a viewing of the film *Jaws* (Director Peter Benchley, 1977) this fear in the real world is a storification effect of the narration.

4) If you watch a documentary, such as *The Story of Steam Power* or *The Story of Medicine*, and it extends your knowledge of the world, this is a storification. Any form of education through story is a storification; even education that is not factual. For example, we emerge from

receiving the film narration of *Back to the Future* fully in the knowledge that it takes 1.21 gigawatts of electricity to power time travel.

This is an interesting one. In considering a narrative, we do not judge it on the basis of its veracity. We judge it purely on whether it makes narrative sense. We judge it on what it *means to us*, not on whether it is true or false. A work of fiction still has meaning. Take the story of Santa Claus. I hate to break it to you, but this is fiction. However, it has narrative logic so is unconsciously and automatically memorised. We decide how to apply and use that story in our real lives by conscious evaluation when that script is pattern-matched against our situation and offered up for consideration. We consciously evaluate a script in terms of the outcomes and implications — for example, the moral context, social norms, personal benefits — and activate, reject or 'edit' the script as we see fit for our own personal mindset. Consider the great religions of the world throughout history. For the sake of argument, let us assume there are 100 religions. All are based on a book of stories. Parables and fables that exemplify good and bad behaviour that can be used to align a society to an ideology that drives ethical behaviour and asserts moral correctness. For the followers of any one of these religions, the book and the stories it contains have meaning so strong that they will lead their lives by them. To the followers of other religions, or no religion, this book has meaning only in the context of the way it drives its followers. A memory is a function of the human logic in a narrative and the inherent meaning, not a function of 'truth' or 'lies'. Thinking along these lines can also be applied, of course, to advertising, political persuasion, and propaganda. It only has to make sense to have meaning, it does not have to be true.

5) Education through vicarious learning is also a storification. If a protagonist takes an action, and that action leads to consequences, the protagonist may or may not learn the lesson of that cause-effect chain (indeed, they may be dead) but the receiver of the story can assimilate the events and relate them to life and actions in their real world. As we have seen already, if a person absorbs a story and —

consciously or unconsciously — lays down a memory that they later use in their own lives, that is a storification effect. For example, a child learning the Heimlich manoeuvre from watching *Spongebob Squarepants* or *Madame Doubtfire*.

6) If a country at war distributes propaganda leaflets to the enemy population or military they are attempting to impact their mindsets. If a person reading the propaganda believes it, and takes action as a result, this is storification. If a person reading the propaganda rejects it, and takes action as a result, this is also storification. The people creating the propaganda are impacting the mindsets and behaviours of the receivers of the text. They are reading it, receiving a narrafication — a narrative that makes sense — and finding meaning in their real lives. This is storification.

7) I have one final example that I think is a clear and simple storification. I am going to tell you a joke:
Two fish in a tank. One says to the other: 'Do you know how to drive this thing?'

Our cultural knowledge and experience initially delivers to our working memory an understanding of what a fish in a tank 'means', and we (perhaps) receive an image of a pair of goldfish in an aquarium. This is the signification. However, later in the sentence the concept of 'driving a tank' causes us to re-evaluate our signification to accommodate the kind of tank that might be driven. Our cultural knowledge and experience of what might represent a tank that can be driven switches the noun to a military tank. However, the original sentence has this tank occupied by two fish. We combine the contents of each logical premise in building the narrafication and receive an incongruous outcome: two fish attempting to drive a military tank. This final narrative in mind, involving two fish having a conversation in a military tank, is new to us, and this is a storification. A new 'worldview' — however trivial or fictional or plain crazy — is able to be created from things that we know and so is a storification. It does not have to be true, it just has to have narrative logic. The incongruity makes us laugh. More detail on this kind of gap in **section 4.4.5.10 — Knowledge Gaps through Comedy**.

If you hear a joke and it makes you laugh, that aural manifestation in the real world and that imagery in mind is a storification. If you go on to repeat that joke, this is evidence of storification as the joke manifests from you in the real world. For some, the joke may not cause humour. The imagery may not match my description. The joke may not storify. However, if someone goes on to tell another that they hated this joke, or it was the worst joke ever, or they ask someone to explain it, these are also examples of storification.

As with the signification examples we experienced earlier, we may feel immune to the effects of storification, however, it is not possible for us to quantify the impact. Indeed, if a narration inspires the assertion of immunity to the effect of the story, that is, in itself, a storification. To consciously reject the implicit meaning of, say, a television advertisement, is to admit it has storified in your mind. You cannot reject the meaning they wish you to inherit if you did not buy the myth in the first place!

Perhaps the best explanation of storification is the result of the relationship between what is evidently a work of fiction and the meaningful memory that emerges from this tissue of lies. When a cartoon narration about a talking sea-sponge called SpongeBob who lives in a pineapple on the seabed, with his Starfish mate and an uptight squid can result in a child in the real world saving the life of a relative, this is the power of a well-crafted story to break out of its fictional roots and storify into becoming a very real part of the mental make-up and drive of the receiver of a story.

These examples cannot be formalised or generalised, so this definition of storification is somewhat nebulous, but that is deliberate on my part. The mind is an esoteric entity, so it seems entirely appropriate that a story — a function of mind — is equally challenging to quantify. Moreover, in terms of academic rigour, attempting to specify the mindset of a receiver or an audience is beyond the scope of this work. It is evident that different people receive different things from a narration, from complete non-comprehension to a glorious personal insight into how a person should live their life, so I am shamelessly avoiding the subject of reception theory and any attempt to specify the mindset of the receiver. My aim is to identify the triggers for story reflexes, but I will not specify the product these triggers inspire. I will address this issue more deeply in the theoretical framework of the next section.

1.6 Summary

This has been a long and complex chapter on linguistics and mental processes. Let's take a moment to summarise the journey we have taken.

The linguistic sign comprises two elements: the signifier in the real world, which manifests as an impact on a receiver's sensory apparatus, and the signified — the phenomenological entity in mind, inspired by pattern-matching the signifier against knowledge in mind. The signified has meaning because of its relationship to other signifieds. A sign only has value when placed into the linguistic system of which it is a part. As Saussure reminded us, a coin does not have value or meaning because of the metal it is made of; it has value because of the human overlaid meaning of that coin within the language of economics and monetary systems (Saussure, 1916, pp.117-118).

Personal history and experience can be overlaid on a signifier in such a way as to 'empty' the signified of its orthodox meaning and fill it with cultural knowledge which renders it as a new 'second level' signifier, known as a signification, imbuing the signifier with a meta-meaning; that is one set in a context of human culture. The clothes a person wears can cause connnotation for those with the cultural knowledge to decode the clothing semiology and overlay the meaning inherent in that clothing. For example, clothing may signify a policeman, priest, nurse, soldier, footballer, and so forth. Their clothing provides signification that gives them a cultural meaning.

Signs and significations are static, but life has a diachronic dimension; that is, change over time is a fundamental component of our existence and the way we define ourselves and our lives. The **events** that define a life not only cause interaction between signs and significations, but become signs and significations in their own right. An event is also a signifier and signification, but with the added dimensional complexity brought by what has already happened within an event and what is likely to come next. An event (or representation of an event) comprising change over time is a **narrative**. However, a narrative has no human meaning until there is a person present to perceive it. When events, objects and actors are linked in a causal chain which makes sense to an individual human receiver, that narrative assimilated into mind is called a **story**. When a capable mind absorbs a narrative, it includes the complications and implications of earlier material in the cause-effect chain and probable/possible projections that comprise or imply future directions and consequences. The meaning of a sign or signification, or event, object or actor is defined not simply through its significations, but also through its interactions and relationships with other signs, and its role in the causal logic of a narrative that makes sense to the receiver. Reading all these elements into a narrative in working memory is called the **narrafication of the sign**.

The memory readily accepts change over time and stores narrative events, known as scripts, in long-term, autobiographical narrative memory. Through repetition, scripts become recognised as entities in themselves, indeed as 'objects' that can be held in mind and, although they are entire narratives, they exist, in a phenomenological context, as objects like any other. An event, such as a war, a childhood or a football match, can be held in mind as a single object.

A person can deploy a narrative script, casting themselves as protagonist in a series of steps or events that will bring a desired outcome in their life, such as a script to make a journey. Human beings live their lives primarily by deploying these known narratives to achieve the predicted outcomes. Through repetition, this becomes a largely unconscious process. When faced with a situation, the unconscious mind offers up the most obvious applicable script to apply. The conscious mind evaluates the script in the context of the prevailing circumstances and chooses the best course of action. As the selected script is enacted, the organism uses perception and cognition to refine progress as it steps through the script. The refinements that are made are to match the situation in the real world reported by core consciousness (the status in the real world) against the expectations set by the steps in the script. The result of running the script plus the updates resulting from continuous monitoring through core consciousness creates a live, real-time cognitive map in working memory that the owner continuously follows, monitors and refines in pursuit of the desired outcome. This is You in Motion. The story of you, unfolding moment by moment.

Human beings attempt to impose a narrative structure on anything and everything through pattern-matching against existing knowledge, and do not feel comfortable that they have a good understanding of an item, person or event until a narrative context for it can be constructed with reliable narrative logic. In negotiating life events, the most commonly used and successful scripts are applied with very little conscious mental effort. However, when a person finds that the running script is incomplete, or has gaps, or takes an unexpected turn, or is in any way no longer fit for purpose, the higher cognitive functions are aroused. The gaps between expectation set by the script and the real-world status reported by core consciousness triggers the higher cognitive functions, which are brought to bear on the narrative disruption to provide knowledge from the protagonist's personal history, cultural understanding, imagination, reasoning and experience to project into those gaps to repair the narrative and achieve the desired outcome via a reconstructed route. Alternatively, the organism might change the narrative through the application of alternative scripts from autobiographical narrative memory. A new narrative, created in mind through the application of intellect in this way, if it is complete and leads to an outcome, will be laid down in long-term memory as a new script and may be triggered in future if its predictable outcome is desired and the situation implies that its application will lead to the benefit that script has been shown to bring. (Equally, if that script leads to a predictable negative outcome, the path it entails will be recognised and diverted or avoided.)

Sir Francis Bacon stated in 1597, 'Knowledge is power'. The implicit truth in this statement makes it reasonable to conclude that human beings naturally thirst for effective narratives that produce beneficial outcomes. There is a primeval atavistic drive for this kind of knowledge because it advances the individual in their survival and promotes that individual's personal chances and the prospects for their genetic line.

I argue that it is with the storification dynamic that we get the overlap of neuroscience with story. A storyteller can provide the narrative framing to inspire a script from autobiographical narrative memory, and they can provide reactions and motivations of characters to trigger a cognitive map from the receiver's core consciousness. Gaps in the resultant narrative, built in working memory, cause writerly work to be done by the receiver, and a complete story in mind results. When writerly work takes place in the production of the story, this is when the receiver takes ownership of the story and creates personal memories that have the power to become a part of that person's mental make-up. This is the process of storification and occurs through the same dynamics when absorbing a story as it does through a real-world experience. That is, gaps that are found in a real-world situation or gaps that are presented by a storyteller in a narration both cause writerly work and both cause new stories to be created which are laid down in long-term autobiographical narrative memory.

In the case of both real-world and fictional narration, it is knowledge gaps in the narrative that trigger the storification to take place. Knowledge gaps are cues for the hermeneutic process — the act of interpretation that changes information from the outside (stimulation to the senses) into knowledge (phenomenological structures in mind). It is the gap that triggers the higher cognitive functions to activate reason, imagination and speculation to fill the gaps and thereby create a story in mind.

And it is all because of the lucky positioning of that innocent little floating bone in your throat.

2   A Theoretical Frame

A good storyteller knows that a fishing net is not made of rope. A fishing net is made of holes. Without the holes, the net would not function or exist.

Before we can develop a useful and comprehensive taxonomy of knowledge gaps, it is necessary to formalise the related terms and dynamics into an epistemological framework. Many of the terms used in narratology have accumulated various or ambiguous meanings, depending upon who you read, and these must be clarified if the constructivist narratology of this book is going to be complete.

2.1   Information and Knowledge

A distinction must be made between information and knowledge to create a clear boundary between narrative and story.

Information is the material that stimulates a human receiver's senses. In nature, this is the raw input data. In constructing a narration, storytellers use communication media to deliver the stream of information to the senses.

In both natural and constructed narrations, the receiver **interprets** this sensory bombardment, transmuting the information received from the outside world across the hermeneutic boundary (hermeneutics is the study of interpretation) into knowledge in mind.

Knowledge is, for the purposes of this book, the assimilated version of information once it is converted into human meaning in mind. That is, phenomenological structures of signs, significations, narrafications and storifications that make logical sense to the receiver.

According to Bordwell, there are three fundamental systems that must be understood for a narrative to make sense. Representation of

time, space and causal logic (Bordwell, 1985a, pp.12-60). All knowledge (and therefore knowledge gaps) must be in the context of these three systems.

A narrative is an information stream. A story is a version of that narrative built in mind through assimilating that information through the prism of human interpretation into knowledge in mind.

There is no knowledge in the material world; only information. Knowledge is only in mind.

There is no story in the material world; only narrative. Story is only in mind.

The receiver takes in the information in its raw sensory form, and by applying their intellect, personal history, experience and cultural knowledge, they turn that information into a narrative-in-mind that makes sense to them. This version of the narrative, a phenomenological entity spawned in mind as a result of receiving the narration and converting it into a meaningful cause-effect chain, is a story. The conversion from information to knowledge may be simplistic, such as pattern-matching a basic linguistic sign, or it may be comprised of highly complex connotations of the abstract storifications that can only be derived once all the information has been assimilated in, say, a two-hour film, a Shakespearean play or classical work of Russian literature.

Looking ahead to how a constructivist approach might become applied in narratology as well as in story industries, one of the key advantages of this separation of information from knowledge is that a knowledge gap has a tangible presence in both the information stream (a material, realist, presence in the real world) and the meaning in mind (an idealist, phenomenological presence). This means that the presence of a knowledge gap is measurable in the denoted material that constitutes the narration. Because the tangible seed of a knowledge gap in the information stream is the trigger for a reflexive mental response (the application of the higher cognitive functions projecting into the gap), each knowledge gap is a pairing of a tangible seed in the information stream with a manifest absence in the causal logic of the story built from knowledge in mind (the knowledge gap itself). As we have established, information and knowledge are not interchangeable terms; however, they are inter-linked components of one dynamic — the conversion of narrative into story — which is at the root of the communication process between a writer and a receiver of story. Whenever there is a knowledge gap, there will be a related causation in the information stream — an information gap, if you will — which can be identified in the denoted text and shown to be facilitating the knowledge gap in mind that triggers story reflexes.

Shortly, I will demonstrate through example that the knowledge gap in the story in mind has its source and trigger in the information stream (the narration). This distinction is key to the validation of a constructivist narratology. Narrative communication takes place on both these two different planes: the information plane (in the real world) and the knowledge plane (in mind). Assuming a work of fiction, the process steps are as follows:

1) The work of fiction begins as a story in the mind of the author, on the knowledge plane.
2) The author converts this into a text that exists as material on the information plane.
3) Communication media deliver this text in the form of a narration to the senses of a receiver. This takes place on the information plane.
4) The receiver of the information stream interprets it into knowledge in mind, on the knowledge plane.

As depicted in figure 9, the order of events runs from Knowledge (Author) —> Information (text) —> Information (senses) —> Knowledge (Receiver). I intend to show how knowledge gaps are the common denominator in the encoding (author) and decoding (receiver) process that communicates knowledge between the author and receiver.

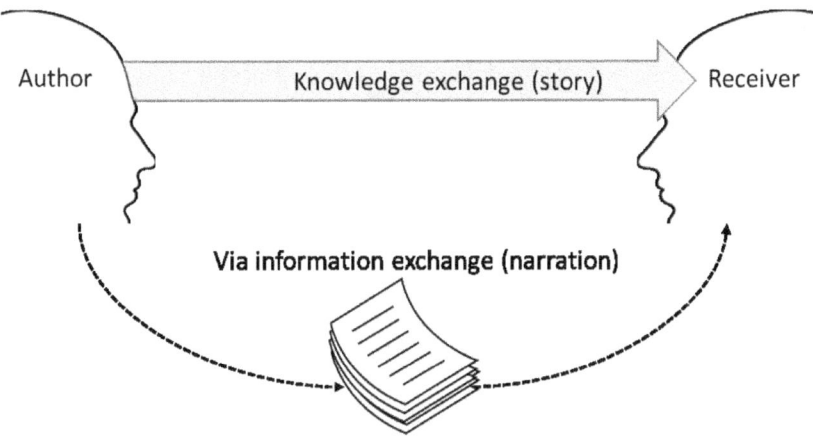

Figure 9: Knowledge versus information exchange

Traditional narratology has focused almost exclusively on the mechanisms and modes of the information plane; specifically on the information transfer between the text and the senses of the receiver. In this work I claim that the *meaningful* communication involves the mechanisms and modes of *knowledge* transfer between two human minds: an author and a receiver.

In a telephone conversation, the *information* passes down the telephone line, facilitated by handsets, cables, media and electronics, but the *knowledge* is exchanged between two human beings. It is this knowledge exchange which is meaningful and can be considered completely independent of the conduit that facilitates the information exchange.

Of course, the media used in the transfer of information is essential, and it has an impact because it changes which of the receiver's senses are most utilised; but this is part of the skill of the media specialists — how to get that knowledge across in the form of information. The knowledge exchange may or may not retain its integrity through the conversion to information in media back into knowledge. Indeed, it is *the* challenge to the author firstly and the media specialists secondly to deliver a narration that retains the intent (author) and integrity (media specialists) of the knowledge transfer.

I argue that it is the knowledge exchange which should be the primary concern of narratology, with the information exchange as one component of the wider discipline. The origin of storytelling was an oral tradition; person-to-person, and the addition of media has simply complicated what must still be considered a person-to-person semiotic/linguistic exchange if narratology is to focus on the meaningful dynamics. I argue that the same dynamic is at play with a book, film, theatre production, comic strip, radio play, ballet, animation — any story form. It is the human-to-human *knowledge* dynamics that embrace story as well as narrative, whereas the *information* exchange between the two humans is a functional component with many variables. The information exchange is concerned primarily with information. At best this creates a narrative — not a story — and is there solely to facilitate the knowledge exchange that does contain the story. If narratology is to embrace narrative *and* story, it must be constructivist in order that it can embrace knowledge as well as information.

2.2 A Constructivist Narratology

> Meaning is not discovered, but constructed.
>
> **Michael Crotty (1998, pp.1-17)**

If it is accepted that narratology is concerned with both the human-to-human *knowledge* exchange (stories) as well as the media, systems and modes of *information* exchange in the material world (narration), then narratology is in the philosophical realm of constructivism. Meaning is not awaiting discovery under stones and in hedges. Knowledge and meaning (and stories) are constructed in mind.

To help create a clear theoretical basis, let us gradually build up a pictorial representation of the delivery of a film narration. In doing so we will define and situate our terms in a constructivist frame. **Figure 10: The Components of Story - 1** is a depiction of narrative information delivered over time — the first layer as we gradually build our picture of the delivery of a film narration.

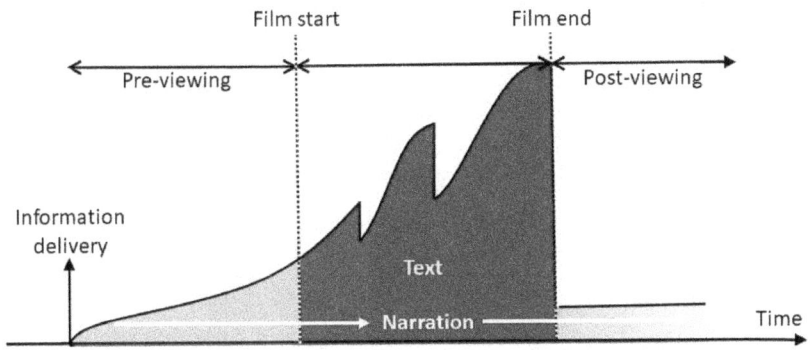

Figure 10: The Components of Story - 1

A narrative involves change over time, so time is represented along the X axis, advancing from left to right. Information is delivered in the form of the narration assaulting the senses of a receiver and is represented by the shaded areas. Increasing quantities of information are shown on the Y axis. There are two types of shaded area because a narration begins before one sits down in the cinema, and continues after it has finished. The 'text' is the formal narrated component delivered to a seated cinema audience. All the narrative information that is not within 'the text itself', is known as **paratext** and **subtext**. Let us explain these elements.

2.2.1 The Text

Reference to the text is to the material that is selected and prepared for delivery, and although 'text' implies words on paper, it is a generic term for the material for narration in any medium. The text is the formally organised information for delivery. The six words of the shortest novel 'For Sale. Baby's Shoes. Never Worn' — that is 'the text' of that novel. The contents of the reel of film that delivers the movie in a cinema screening — that pre-prepared, specific information is 'the text'. As the text is delivered, this is the formal narration, and the period of delivery into which the receiver is expected to become immersed in the story world is the diegesis. The text is the material for delivery, the narration is the real-time delivery (the 'telling' of the story), and the receiver is said to become immersed in the diegesis. (More on diegesis and mimesis shortly.)

2.2.2 Paratext

As can be seen in **Figure 10: The Components of Story – 1** the narration begins before the delivery of the text itself. Indeed, the narration begins before the receiver of the film enters the cinema or a reader lays a hand on the book. As soon as we become aware of a story's potential existence, and as we build knowledge of the upcoming film through its stars and through the information in the poster, advertisements, merchandise, trailers, reviews and so on, the narration is underway. The narration also continues after the text itself has ended. These elements that precede and surround the viewing are called the **Paratext**.

Everything tangible that goes around the text, but is not the text, and yet could be considered a part of the narration, is paratext. I use the word 'tangible' here to separate the paratext from the subtext. Paratext is material information, existing in the real world, as distinct from subtext that is knowledge created in mind. We shall address subtext later.

As Jonathan Gray puts it in his work on paratext entitled *Show Sold Separately*:

> Paratexts are the greeters, gatekeepers and cheerleaders for and of the media, filters through which we must pass on our way to 'The Text Itself'. (Gray, 2010, p.17)

It is the same for other media. When fans of Harry Potter, who had absorbed several books and films already, found out that there was a new Harry Potter book coming out, they knew an awful lot about it before it was in their hands. There is a great deal of paratext surrounding JK Rowling, her characters and the world she created. Does a person know what to expect when there is a new *Jack Reacher* book or *James Bond* film coming along? A new *Star Wars* movie? A television show, like *Family Guy* or *The Simpsons*, or your favourite soap opera? Many films and books are preceded and accompanied by extraordinary quantities of paratext, some of which is carefully crafted and managed (such as the marketing), and some of which is coincidental (such as the behaviour of fans or even the stars in the real world). From a formal viewpoint, paratext is a component of the narration, and the story in your head has begun to develop long before you get to 'the text itself'. Earlier in this book, I mentioned how a lady fainted and fell down some stairs during a screening. Her fall became part of the narration (whether we liked it or not) because it became part of the information stream, and because it was extra-diegetic (that is, it was not part of 'the text') it was paratext. Note also that this paratext occurred during the delivery of the text itself. In this respect, my diagram is slightly incorrect, because paratext can be delivered during the formal narration, not only before and after the delivery of 'the text itself'.

Similarly, once the text has finished, the story in your mind is likely to change and develop after you have left the cinema, lost the book or long since stopped thinking about it. A story is never set in stone. As the stars continue to manifest in society and their images change; as you grow and feel differently through your own maturity or other cultural influences; as you encounter merchandise, DVD extras and linked video games; as you are exposed to sequels and other versions of the story — the narration is never over. The story — and do not forget, the story is not the narration, the story is only ever the unique production in your mind — will change over time as you change and as the elements of the story that appear in your life re-emerge. I feel sure you can think of a story that you used to love, then much later, the discovery that one of the stars is, say, a paedophile, had a profound effect on your feelings about the story. The text itself has not changed, but the narration has continued and evolved for you because of the star's behaviours, and your story, in your own mind, is now changed. This is all the effect of paratext as a component of the narration.

2.2.3 Subtext

While the text and paratext constitute all the information that makes the narration in the information realm, subtext is the term for the knowledge that the receiver of the story contributes to the narrative in mind for themselves. A story effectively has two sources of knowledge in mind: the knowledge delivered by the author (signifiers and narrafications) and the knowledge provided by the receiver for themselves (signifieds, significations and storifications).

To put this another way, a story comprises two things in mind: the interpreted narration as it builds in working memory (readerly work) and the knowledge that goes into the gaps (writerly work).

When there is a gap in knowledge, subtext is the knowledge that goes into the gaps. There is a subtext in the signifier 'ROSE'. The knowledge that goes into the gap is the connotated understanding of love, romance and courtship. This is the subtext in the rose. Exponentially more complex gaps are implicit to narrafications, requiring significant writerly work from the receiver. The work done is to deliver the subtext into the knowledge gaps.

Subtext completes the story. Subtext is the knowledge delivered into the narrative-in-mind by the receiver of a narration from their own cultural history and experience. I will look more deeply at subtext later, because clearly, as it is the knowledge that goes into the gaps, it is *ipso facto* critical to the function of knowledge gaps. For the moment, to put it simply, subtext is the knowledge that goes into a knowledge gap.

2.2.4 The Story

As we know, the narration assaults the senses of a receiver, and they construct a story in mind as a result. Let us add some more terms to our diagram and include the story that is inspired into mind by receiving the narration.

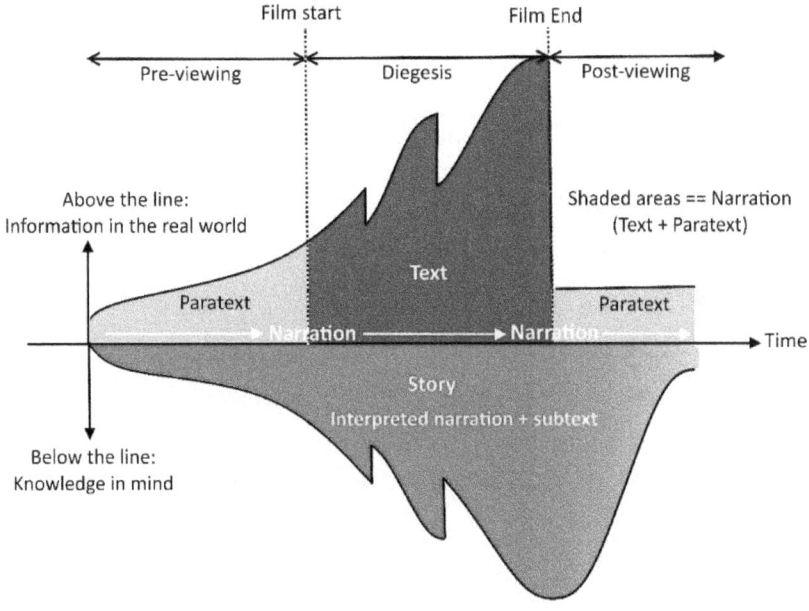

Figure 11: The Components of Story - 2

Information is above the line. Knowledge is below the line. The real world is above the line. The world in mind is below the line. Narration is 'above the line' (the blue shaded areas). The story is 'below the line' (the red shaded area). So, as the narration progresses in the real world (change over time) the story is inspired into mind. This separation brings us two more terms. Simplistically put, they are the syuzhet (everything above the line) and the fabula (everything below).

2.2.5 Syuzhet and Fabula

In the 1920s, the Russian formalists (notably, Boris Tomashevsky, Viktor Shklovsky and Vladimir Propp) argued that every narrative can be divided into two components which they termed the **syuzhet** and the **fabula**. There have been many translations and interpretations of their work, of which mine is but one tailored for my constructivist epistemology, and I invite you to read the Scheffel, M. (2013) article on *Narrative Constitution* for a fulsome discussion of the many available authoritative opinions on these terms.

In this work I find support for my constructivist epistemology from authorities such as Barthes and Genette who also drew up their narratological models against the background of Saussure's theory of the linguistic sign and treat the difference between syuzhet and fabula as an extended and more complex version of the dichotomy between the signifier and signified. In this reading, the syuzhet is the arrangement of information. The fabula is the arrangement of knowledge in mind as a result of receiving and interpreting syuzhet material.

For my epistemology, the term syuzhet identifies the empirical: everything that is known and denoted which *could possibly* form a relevant part of a narration. It is the entire armoury of information available to the author in the construction of a text. The narration itself is a subset of the syuzhet, that is, the narration is the material selected from the syuzhet that is actually delivered in a specific telling. The plot is a plan for a narration. The selection of material from the syuzhet — the events and the order in which they will be presented — in preparation for delivering a narration. More on plot shortly.

The term fabula refers to all possible *interpretations* of the presented syuzhet material. However, no receiver of a narration in any given medium will apprehend all possible interpretations, so the term 'story' is used to refer to the specific, individual phenomenon created in the mind by an individual receiver of a narration. A story is therefore a subset of the fabula; the individual's specific interpretation-in-mind of the received syuzhet information. The syuzhet is information, the fabula is knowledge. The syuzhet is everything above the line; the fabula is all possible interpretation below the line. The narration is a subset of the syuzhet and the story is a subset of the fabula.

This gives rise to some fascinating considerations. Firstly, The Russian formalists considered the differences between the syuzhet and the fabula to be a measure of the 'literariness' of the work. That is, the greater the differences, the finer the work is considered to be. Secondly, notice that whilst the fabula can be readily understood as the interpretation of syuzhet material, it can equally be seen as resident in the mind of the author before he or she begins the work of creating the syuzhet. The author begins with a fabula in their own mind, uses syuzhet material as the tools from which to create a text, and if they do a good enough job, and the receiver is capable of the readerly and writerly work, then the receiver of the narration will receive a subset of the fabula from the syuzhet material used to create the narration, and that fabula material should be a representative version of the originally selected fabula material that composed the story in the mind of the author in the first place.

Knowledge Gaps

Knowledge gaps integral to the syuzhet (gaps seeded in the information above the line) *cause* the fabula (knowledge below the line) to be constructed because it is the knowledge gaps that trigger connotation and writerly work. Every signified in the syuzhet has a potential signifier in the fabula. Every sign its potential signification. Every narrafication event in the syuzhet its corresponding storification in the fabula. The way the information is crafted from the myriad of options in the syuzhet causes the knowledge gaps that inspire interpretation and thereby generate fabula entities. It is the craft of a story creator to select objects and events from the syuzhet and present them skilfully enough that they trigger enough knowledge in mind for the receiver of the narration to derive a cohesive version of the fabula in mind. The craft referred to here is plotting. Creating a plan for a narration.

The X axis in our diagram is a boundary between information and knowledge. Knowledge gaps embedded in the information stream trigger the mental reflexes that cause interpretation and therefore fabula material is inspired into mind and the story is gradually constructed.

The content of the narration causes interpretation and that interpretation happens because of the knowledge gaps that must be filled to turn information into knowledge. Narration into story. Syuzhet into fabula.

It is interesting to note that in all but the simplest of narrations, none of these elements of story can be specified. The complete syuzhet and the complete fabula are too large to specify and their contents change over time even if the text does not change. Every story is a personal version of the fabula, which includes facets of the receiver's personality, gender, conditioning, history, age and so forth, so it is unique to each recipient of a narration, and these personal factors will also change over time. Every individual narration includes an unspecifiable quantity of paratext to which the individual receiver is exposed, so every story is a unique production-in-mind. Even a specific individual's story in mind also changes with time as they change and learn and gain new experience.

This is a salutary point to make. Stories are not amenable to scientific deconstruction. They are an art form and can never be reduced to logic, proofs and absolutes. Despite all my efforts to uncover their secrets, it is pleasing to know that stories will, ultimately always retain a level of mystery. It is also interesting to note that Damasio came to the same conclusion after his life's work as a brain scientist: "The mystery of consciousness remains a mystery" (Damasio, 2010, p.262). The fabula will always be beyond precise specification, therefore, so will the syuzhet.

The only unchanging component in the story chain is the specific diegetic delivery; that is, the 'text itself'; the words in the book or, in the film example, the screened part of the narration (excluding the paratext). The words in a book are not changed through reading them. The text of any single film screening is essentially the same on every transmission, even though the complete narration will vary on every occasion and for every individual because of their personal knowledge, experience, gender, age and so on (that is, the subtext they bring), and the paratext to which they are exposed.

In this respect, the terms syuzhet and fabula have a specific use. As has been discussed, it is not possible to specify the mindset of the author in their creative activities, and it is not possible to specify the mindset of the receiver. However, because the terms syuzhet and fabula embrace everything of relevance, they can be used to generically refer to all elements that may be a part of the narration (that is, they may feasibly have been a part of the author's mindset) and — most usefully — the fabula can be used to refer to phenomena that may feasibly be part of the receiver's story in mind. A researcher therefore only needs to derive a phenomenological entity in their own mind to be sure it can validly be considered a component of the fabula. They did it, so it is possible. In this way, referring to 'fabula' (general) rather than 'story' (specific) will generally be a valid assertion of receiver behaviour.

2.2.6 The Hermeneutic Boundary

Hermeneutics is the study of interpretation. The original thinking in this book comes from the re-centring of narratology at the hermeneutic boundary — the point at which information in the real-world assaults the senses and becomes interpreted into knowledge in mind. (The X axis on our illustration is the hermeneutic boundary.) When interpretation takes place, this is the critical moment when a person with appropriate cultural knowledge and personal history experiences the unconscious reflex of connotation. When a person sees the picture of the rose in **Figure 2 - Signification**, it arrives at their senses as information (a flower) and crosses the hermeneutic boundary to become knowledge in mind. A representation of a rose out there in the material world instantly becomes a phenomenological context in mind concerned with romance and courtship. The hermeneutic boundary is the bridge between information in the outside world assaulting the human senses, and the knowledge in mind that results from interpreting these stimuli.

The Bridge Across the Hermeneutic Boundary

Throughout this work, I have referred to the information gap/knowledge gap relationship as a *reflexive* dynamic, and you may be feeling this is not right, because it appears to run in one direction, from information to knowledge, where a reflexive dynamic involves a circular dependency. Where is the return path on this reflexivity – the dependency in the other direction from the knowledge to information? It is here that the traditional failing of narratology is highlighted. Because the circuit is indeed present, however, it does not begin from the information.

To include a full cycle, as I contend must happen to encompass a complete narratology, we must begin at the beginning with the creative phase of production and the author. The gap in the information stream was crafted into place by the author as a function of the knowledge (story) they have in mind to begin with. The author begins with a story, and the narrative they create to represent that story in textual form comprises two types of element, like a fishing net: denoted material and information gaps, and both these elements require interpretation. As the receiver of the narration interprets the information into knowledge, the gaps in the information stream convert into gaps in the knowledge stream; gaps that are filled by the writerly work of the receiver. Thus, reflexive it is, running from knowledge (author) to information (text) and then back to knowledge again (receiver), albeit that the knowledge component of the circular definition resides in two different minds.

The recognition and acceptance of a reflexive relationship between information in narrative and meaning in mind (story) is implicit acceptance that narratology is currently poorly grounded in narrative structuralism. Narratology is more complete when considered constructivist in its philosophical foundation in order to include knowledge (and therefore story). This also implies that all the work in traditional narratology is still valuable and included. A constructivist narratology embraces the traditional, because it includes the information, the text and the media, however it extends narratology to include story and mind as well as narrative and structure.

2.2.7 Modes of Narration

Earlier in this book, we mentioned how, in a philosophical sense, narrative is not meaningful unless there is a human mind to receive it. Narration is therefore all about the tools and methods for delivering an information stream to the senses of a receiver. The narrational voice can change from one narration to another, indeed, from one moment to another within the same narration, but in every *meaningful* communication (and therefore every narration) there is a mode of narration and a receiver.

The positioning of the narrational voice is known as **mediacy**. Genette (1980) asserts that mediacy involves addressing two questions: "Who speaks?" And "who sees?" He identified two fundamental narrational positions: **heterodiegetic** and **homodiegetic** to situate the narrator ("who speaks?"). The heterodiegetic narrational position is a narrator other than a character, and the homodiegetic narrational position is a character within the diegesis. Genette also developed the concept of 'focalisation' to address the question "who sees?" (Genette, 1980, pp.188-194).

There is much discussion of mediacy and focalisation in the literature (cf. Stanzel [1955]; Genette [1980] and Chatman [1978]). Within the context of a constructivist approach, these are facets of the information stream, and their modes can change from one moment to the next during a narration irrespective of which narrational position is adopted. However, the meaningful conversation is taking place between the author and the receiver, not the text and the receiver, so for epistemological purposes, all narrational modes are simply different flavours of information delivery; concerned with the method whereby denoted material in the real world is delivered to the sensory apparatus of the receiver of the narration. A narrator can hold or withhold knowledge, so a type of knowledge gap will be captured in the context of the narrational mode as and when they occur.

When we come to the taxonomy, the way knowledge gaps through narrational mode are contrived will be detailed (see **section 4.4.3.2 - Knowledge gaps through Self-Conscious Narrator**). I do not intend to go deeper into these areas. For the constructivist narratology, I will limit our studies to two modes of narration delineated by Aristotle, known as the Diegetic and the Mimetic.

2.2.7.1 Diegesis and Mimesis

A mimetic narration comprises actors delivering the story through the actions and words of the characters they play, as if a spectator is watching the characters living out the real-time events of their lives in the story world. A diegetic narration has a narrational mode separate from the characters living and moving in their story world, 'telling' the story through a particular medium, such as a narrator *describing* the events as distinct from actors *dramatising* events. A mimesis 'shows' what happens; a diegesis 'tells' what happens.

> The poet may imitate by narration — in which he can either take another personality as Homer does or speak in his own person unchanged — or he may present all his characters as living and moving before us (Aristotle [~335BC], 1961, p.5).

Strictly speaking, although mimesis is delivered by the characters in their story world, it is still a method of *telling* the story, so the diegesis continues throughout the mimesis. That is, the diegesis is the period of the narration that is narrated (the delivery of the text itself. In simple terms, the diegesis is the bit between 'once upon a time' and 'they all lived happily ever after'), and the mimesis is a subset of the diegesis, that part which is delivered through the characters living and moving before us.

It is interesting to observe that, when receiving a narration, a receiver exists on two different story planes. They exist as normal in the real-world, and at the same time they experience a sense of immersion in the story world. The diegesis is used to refer to the proportion of the narration that is potentially 'immersive'. While the poster for the musical, or the back-cover 'blurb' of a novel, or the actions of a film star in their real lives, or the title and trailer for the film do form part of the narration, they are not part of the diegesis, because they are not narrated. They are not part of a specific delivery of 'the text itself'. In my work, when I refer to the diegesis, my intention is to refer to the part of the narration that is intended to immerse the receiver in the story world. Some parts of this may be mimetic, some diegetic, but the diegesis is the entire part of the narration that is the delivery of 'the text itself' and is intended to cause immersion.

This distinction also asserts that the 'real world' is an information-based existence, and the story world is a knowledge-based existence. The narration is the delivery of information to the senses of the receiver, however, the receiver immerses themselves into the story world *through* the narration, and as they do, there emerges a difference between the information and the story that is built in mind. This difference is recognised in the distinction between the narration and the diegesis. A receiver remembers the story of *Little Red Riding Hood* but does not remember the words that composed that story. In this sense, the receiver 'enters the diegesis' (immerses themselves in the story world), rather than 'receives the narration' (reads the words or receives the screening). In many ways, this entire book is about this subtle distinction.

2.3 The Theoretical Framework — Summary

All of which allows us to complete our illustration with all the terms we have addressed.

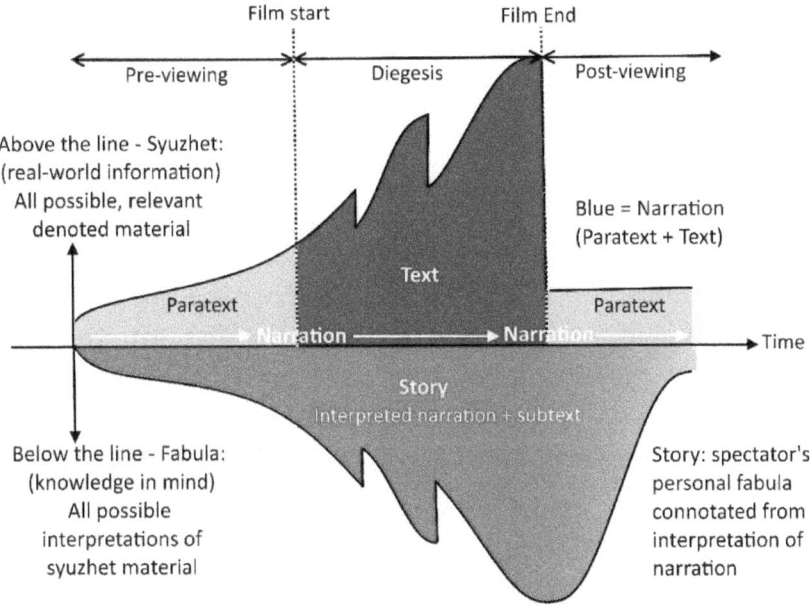

Figure 12: The Components of Story

The syuzhet is the term for the maximal set of information elements that could feasibly be used in the narration. The syuzhet is everything in this set from which a subset is chosen by the author in the creation of the text.

The Plot

The plot is the selection of syuzhet elements and the order in which they are to be delivered — a plan for a narration. A plan to deliver a stream of information. The text is the content of that plot that will be delivered to the receiver — in the case of a film, the text is the content of the reel of film that creates the screening itself. Different syuzhet material can be selected for delivery, creating a different plot for what is essentially the same story. Think how many versions there have been of, for example, Sherlock Holmes stories. The stories remain essentially the same although different syuzhet materials

— different representations of time, space and causal logic — are selected and ordered for each reimagining.

The real-time delivery of the text is the diegetic component of the narration during which the receiver is actively drawn into the story world. Within the narration, the mimesis is a subset of the diegesis; the component of the narration that is delivered by the characters moving and interacting in their story world. So, for example, the title sequence, the narrator's voice-over and the musical score are part of the diegesis, but are not part of the mimesis. The actions and words of a character are the mimesis, but are also a form of narration, so are part of the diegesis.

The paratext is all syuzhet material that precedes (before), augments (during) and extends (after) the narration beyond the planned text. Someone's mobile phone ringing during the screening is paratext; it is, unfortunately, part of the specific narration. Further paratext extends the narration long into the future after the screening, as the receiver thinks about the subtext and storifications, is exposed to video games, merchandise or sequels, or finds a reason to alter their opinion of one of the stars of the film due to their behaviour in the real world.

The syuzhet is all possible relevant signifiers that might be used in a narration of this story, and the fabula is all possible interpretations of the delivered syuzhet material. Thus, the narration is a subset of the syuzhet and the story is a subset of the fabula; a story is a personal fabula, unique to this individual receiver.

Storytelling is a knowledge transfer between an author and a receiver; the transfer of a fabula in the author's mind to a version of that fabula in the mind of the receiver. The receiver of the narration does readerly work (interpretation) and writerly work (providing subtext) to create a version of the fabula in mind (a story).

3 A Through-line from History

In order to situate this work appropriately, it is useful to understand some of the history. I have focussed primarily on cinema, because it is cinema that has developed from nothing into a dominant narrative art form over the last 120 years. Cinema not only has a comprehensively documented development history but also has a glut of 'how to write' books and gurus that show how analytical thinking has developed alongside the art. It is also within scriptwriting that the most prevalent form of formulaic storytelling has become embedded into the DNA of production, providing a good example of how narratology manifests in the creative arts.

Contemporary scriptwriting manuals generally source their foundations from what Bordwell (1985b) calls 'canonical story format', a set of structural imperatives which he describes as being at the core of 'classical Hollywood narrative'. In summary, they are as follows:

- Introduction of setting and characters.
- Setting of protagonist goal(s).
- Actions to achieve goals complicated by obstacles and conflict.
- Climax and resolution.

(Bordwell, 1985b, pp.34,35)

These canons were fully established and operational by 1917, which is less than twenty years after the first films were made and yet — importantly — still more than a decade before the inception of synchronised sound. These principles have remained at the centre of script guidance ever since:

> In formal design, today's Hollywood cinema is largely continuous with yesterday's; [built on] conventions that are as powerful today as they were in 1960, or 1940, or 1920. Once we get past generalizations about blockbusters and postmodern fragmentation, we find a lot that adheres to very old canons. (Bordwell, 2006, p.35)

Kristin Thompson investigated the formulation of norms of narrative and stylistic structure in Hollywood during the transitional years between 1909 and 1917; the period in which these canons were established. Thompson points out that early films and principles, from which the classical Hollywood narrative grew, were founded in vaudeville and in the theatre of the late nineteenth century. Early filmmakers assumed the point-of-view of a seated spectator looking at a stage, resulting in a single-shot film from a fixed camera. Many of the earliest presentations were indeed filmed screenings of vaudeville acts and skits, and, of course, had no synchronous sound or dialogue (Thompson, 1985, pp.174-179). Under these conditions, the earliest films were necessarily built upon action, rather than character. Practical jokes, trick films (such as disappearance through a basic edit), skits and silent comedy routines were commonplace. Later in this period, as film-making generally (and editing specifically) became more sophisticated, more complex but still action-focused films emerged, based around incidents such as a fight or a chase.

It is interesting to consider how writing manuals might be different today if the foundational principles included factors which were not available to the early filmmakers, such as the nuance of close-ups and sophisticated editing, the highly significant contribution of dialogue and sound, and roots that were not so firmly set in theatre. Even today, contemporary guidance for writers talks about 'acts' and 'scenes' because these are the tangible elements of representation derived from the theatre, Originally functions of the need to change sets and scenery, later reinforced by the length of a reel of film in those early days these factors were, by extension, applied to early film. These imperatives are for the medium, not for story creation; they are the manipulation of information; the concern of the media expert, not of the story creator. Novelists were there a long time before cinema and have no such limitations. They write without the strictures of the presentation medium, set-changes, stage direction; acts, scenes and their associated restrictions; nor the limiting effect of 'guidance' for scriptwriters. It is interesting that to this day, novels are often the source of the most highly acclaimed film stories, created without all this 'help'. I argue that this is no coincidence and is directly due to novelists not being restricted by the means of narrative representation and the accepted wisdom inherent to the guidance that goes with scriptwriting. Once the story is written, it is the role of the medium specialists to use their expertise to narrate that story in the context of their medium. This is an important and highly skilled discipline, but one that is separate from the work of the story creator.

Nonetheless, at some point in the development process, after the story has been written, the specific medium does have to be considered, and in the early days of cinema limitations on the medium and the technology were far more severe than they later came to be. It is for these reasons, during the main period of development of classical Hollywood narrative (1909-1917), that novels or short stories were adapted in ways which emphasised action over character, and the commercial guidance of the time reflected the need for such emphasis. Thompson describes how film studios in this period employed staff writers in 'scenario departments', who would adapt a short story or novel for a film narrative by creating a synopsis of the plot which would form the starting point of the film-development process. The scenario department staff writers were restricted by the means of presentation at that time, necessarily focusing on action without nuance, and it was at this time and with these restrictions that a proliferation of scriptwriting manuals emerged, and the foundations for all subsequent guidance were laid.[1]

Films were plot-led, and action driven. Character development was minimal. In film, a scriptwriter must look on his characters from the outside. His viewpoint is a camera lens, and the tools for revealing the mindset of a character are far more limited than those of a novelist, who can readily take a viewer inside the mind of a character and communicate their thoughts, feelings and motivations. Subtle character development remains challenging today but was particularly so in 1905.

> Since the [film] story-writer had limited time to create characters, they must be immediately striking and colourful, developing swiftly if at all, and that development must be hastened by striking

---

[1] For example, Esenwein and Chambers, The Art of Story-Writing (Springfield, Mass.: Home Correspondence School, 1913); Hamilton, C. A Manual of the Art of Fiction (New York: Doubleday, 1918); Woodbridge, E. The Drama: Its Laws and its Techniques (Boston: Allyn & Bacon, 1898); Archer, W. Play-Making: A Manual of Craftsmanship (Boston: Small, Maynard and Co., 1912).

> circumstances. [...] In the classical cinema, our first impressions tend to be lasting ones, and the characters seldom have a complex set of traits. In the novel, on the other hand, character development was considered paramount. [...] Early classical form could hardly hope to create characters as complex as those of the Victorian novel. (Thompson, 1985, pp.170-172)

The focus on action rather than character necessitated by these early restrictions set the tone for all that followed, and the focus on spectacle never left the frame from then until now. It is upon canonical story form, from 100 years ago, that contemporary scriptwriting manuals are built. As Bordwell explains:

> By 1917 American filmmakers had synthesized [early narrative principles] into a unified style, and it was this style, within the next decade, that was taken up and developed around the world. [...] The plots rely on physical movement, vigorous conflicts, escalating dramatic stakes, and a climax driven by time pressure. The visual style, contoured to maximize dramatic impact, is likewise easily understood. [In more recent times, a] few filmmakers have recast familiar forms in more experimental shapes, but even here the tradition is not rejected in toto. A filmmaker who innovates in one respect tends to hold other elements constant. [...] Day by day, creative minds find fresh ways to actualize premises that have proven their effectiveness for nearly a hundred years of moviemaking (Bordwell, 2006, pp.13, 21).

The stubbornness and resilience of these canons is possibly the most surprising aspect. Technical advances through the twentieth century were used to develop character, but not as much as they were used to ramp up the action and create ever-more impressive spectacle that continues to this day. Thomas Schatz suggests that with the advent of big budget, blockbuster films through the 1970s, productions became "increasingly plot-driven, increasingly visceral, kinetic, and fast-paced, increasingly reliant on special effects, increasingly 'fantastic' (and thus apolitical), and increasingly targeted at younger audiences" (Schatz, 1993, p.23).

Successive generations of scriptwriters have learned these same canons and perpetuated a focus on plot and action, giving secondary consideration to those elements of story which embrace nuanced and sophisticated characters; the internal conflicts, thought processes, insecurities, causality and motivation, dilemmas and psychology, their moral drives, subterfuges, knowledge gaps, subtext and hidden ambitions. Such elements are harder to establish and represent in film than in written text, and — importantly — challenging to represent in script-writing guidance. However, there are mechanisms to do so. For example, a narrator can deliver the thoughts and feelings of a character (indeed, a narrator can *be* a character, and thereby communicate their visually hidden mental state). A filmed scenario, such as a character on a counsellor's couch, can pour out their innermost thoughts and feelings in dialogue. Flashbacks can be used to reveal a frame of mind. For example, in the film *Saving Mr Banks* (2013, directed by J.L. Hancock) the flashbacks to the childhood trauma of P.L. Travers (the writer of *Mary Poppins*) explain her motivation — the mental suffering that drives her anxieties and attitude towards Walt Disney (Tom Hanks) in adulthood. Such mechanisms, however, only became possible after the advent of sound in the 1930s, long after the classical Hollywood narrative rule-base for stories had become entrenched with its action-driven imperatives. Even the most recent Hollywood scriptwriting guidance affords less space to aspects of character and maximum attention to structure, action and conflict. The most recent advances in terms of the internet, streaming and digital channels have, on the one hand, brought to life new, agile television production companies eager to take advantage of lowering costs of production and hundreds of routes to market to make fresh, compelling stories that are character driven (because actors are cheaper than effects!); but on the other hand, film piracy has caused Hollywood to go in the opposite direction. Advances in technology have been used to create even more spectacular productions, at astronomically high cost, because Hollywood knows that pirates cannot steal the 'experience' of massive spectacle, 3D and 4D presentations and so on. Yet again, advances in technology have been used to increase action and spectacle rather than character and nuance.

3.1 The Rise of the Structuralist

Thus, the story development advice that adorns our bookshelves today originated in Hollywood, becoming established by around 1917 — the beginning of the period Bordwell describes as 'Classical Hollywood Cinema' (Bordwell, *et al*, 1985a). The film-making corporations that monopolised Hollywood through the 20th century were those which most successfully systemised the end-to-end film development process, and storytelling was not excluded from systemisation. A bi-product was the entrenchment of the 'classical Hollywood narrative' (Bordwell, 1985b, pp.34,35); a codified method of story delivery in terms of chronology, causal links between events, the story-world created, the characters and their agency in the narrative process, and the continuity style of editing that came to characterise the period known as 'classical Hollywood style' (Bordwell *et al*, 1985a).

This systemisation included the development of a set of structural imperatives for story creation. The study of narrative has generally involved taking popular texts and using structuralist principles to deconstruct them in order to establish common universals. As these commonalities were established, they were used to create a model for story development; the logic being that if these common structural elements are constituent parts of a persuasive number of popular stories, then any new story that is structured along similar lines will surely be equally excellent. The result is a formula for story which some writers like (because it gives them a pattern to follow); some writers do not like (because it means bending their story to fit, and thereby removing creative integrity); and which the business side of story industries likes very much, because systemisation gives them objective criteria to use in the evaluation of a story's commercial potential, and a rule base they can apply in managing writers, creative teams and a production procedure that is systemised from end-to-end.

In contemporary production companies, a tick-box mentality is likely to be applied to all feature film submissions arriving at their 'story department', which might look something like this (drawn from various sources):

1) Is the overall script between 90 and 120 pages in length?
2) Does the author establish a location and time setting by page 3?
3) Do I know the protagonist by page 10?
4) Is there an inciting incident that raises a key question in my mind by page 30?

5) Is the key question raised in act 1 answered satisfactorily by the action at climax?
6) Is there a turning point in the life of the protagonist which identifies the end of act 1, spins his world out of balance and sets them off in a new and unexpected direction?
7) Does this turning point identify the quest of the protagonist?
8) Does this quest represent the spine of the whole story? Is it achieved/failed clearly at climax?
9) Are there identifiable forces of antagonism?
10) Does the antagonism stand in clear opposition to the quest of the protagonist?
11) Are the aims of protagonism and antagonism mutually exclusive? (Only one can win, and it inevitably will be at the expense of the other.)
12) Is there a mid-act turning point around page 60 which dramatically changes the fortunes of the protagonist and throws the likelihood of a positive outcome into significant doubt?
13) By the end, are the fortunes/values/morals of the protagonist notably changed through the events of the story?

You get the idea. There may be many more criteria in a complete list, including criteria on the commercial side, providing indication of, for example, genre and sub-genre, the likely audience profile, broad cost of production, the period and location, and the all-important title and logline. However, there are many excellent stories, including Oscar winners and some of the most popular films ever made, which are likely to have been rejected had this kind of tick-box mentality been applied. I suggest that, for example, *Hugo* (2011, directed by Martin Scorsese); *Atonement* (2007, directed by Joe Wright); *Memento* (2000, directed by Christopher Nolan); *Pulp Fiction* (1994, directed by Quentin Tarantino); *Amélie* (2001, directed by Jean-Pierre Jeunet); *Léon: The Professional* (1994, directed by Luc Besson); *Eternal Sunshine of the Spotless Mind* (2004, directed by Michael Gondry); and *The Royal Tanenbaums* (2001, directed by Wes Anderson), to name but a few, would not fit the criteria.

The formulaic model has been built up over more than 100 years, with many of its principles set down during the earliest days of film-making. A procedural, systemised approach may seem fine — inevitable, even. However, the foundations that dominate today were put down in an age before sound, dialogue and sophisticated editing. They are built upon a strong bias towards action and spectacle rather than character development and nuance. Those principles have passed on, relatively unchanged, through generations of scriptwriters. Of course, there are plenty of stories which are genuinely very good and do obey the 'rules'. However, from a narratological perspective, this model is fundamentally flawed in its conception. Why? Because there are exceptions; any story development in media other than film cannot readily use this guidance; and even a film narrative that falls outside of the rigid structural imperatives (such as one of short duration) cannot make use of the system. As a comprehensive, authoritative model for narrative theory, the Hollywood formula cannot be valid, because it can only ever be applicable to a narrow range of stories in a single medium.

It is also interesting to consider that the structural imperatives have been around for so long, and have become so pervasive and definitive in Hollywood, that they are now an accepted part of the cinema experience not just for writers, directors and producers, but for audiences as well. Every mainstream movie-goer alive today has been brought up on a steady diet of the Hollywood formula. The structural imperatives are encoded into the DNA of the vast majority of Hollywood films and, by extension, the DNA of everyone who writes, makes or receives a Hollywood film. Anything that steps outside of the accepted encoding is called 'art house' or 'experimental' or even 'counter cinema'. Part of the problem we have in trying to set ourselves free as contemporary storytellers and filmmakers is that there is such a strong compulsion to encode in the accepted, orthodox way because it brings comfort to those looking to invest *and* to those looking to go to the cinema and simply decode. The next multiplex blockbuster will have a similar underlying structure to all the others, because that is what is safe for the business side and that is what is expected by the audience. This is why I refer to this systemisation as a self-perpetuating circle. The system becomes institutionalised in the mindset of each new generation of filmmakers **and** audiences. Breaking the rules becomes harder with each generation, and those that have tried have been surprised just how embedded these pre-sets and expectations are. Critics who agitate for change are the first to complain about a new film and give it low ratings if it does not fit the established norms. People seem to want change, but then are unlikely to embrace it when it comes.

3.2 Contemporary Guidance

By way of representative example of the Hollywood formula driving guidance to writers, Viki King wrote one of the best-selling recent books on screenwriting: *How to Write a Movie in 21 Days* (King, 2001). King's focus is almost exclusively on the structural elements that she asserts are necessary to good film stories, so she prescribes a rigid structure, based on three acts and a series of events that must happen to the protagonist. For example:

> The event that happens on page 30 throws your character a curve. He is forced to respond or react [...] He decides on a goal to pursue because of what has happened. He is now going about making a plan and implementing it. Let's see the page-30 event that he is forced to respond to. Then let's see what he plans to do about it [...] By page 75 it looks like all is lost; there's even a scene where your hero is about to give up. But then something happens that changes everything: an event that gives him a chance at a goal he didn't even know he had. Think of such an event and write it on card #7. (King, 2001, p.43)

In likening screenplay management to pegging a tablecloth on a clothesline, King's book has similar directions for pegging structural events on pages 1, 3, 10, 30, 45, 60, 75, 90 and 120 of the script.

The problem with these kinds of structural imperatives is that the word 'character' is missing. So is subtext, knowledge gap, morality, learning, privilege and revelation; character growth, metaphor, anagnorisis and peripeteia, cultural allusion and more (all explored in detail later), to say nothing of the innumerable wonderful stories that do not even have three acts, cynically-positioned turning points, overt inciting incidents, and all the rest of it. There are fine stories without a quest for the protagonist, a major dramatic question and barely any conflict at all. And yet writers are given this jelly mould and informed that their story must be this shape if they want it to be any good (and especially if they want to get a deal).

And if that is not cynical enough, the creator of the story, and their development process, is not included in this scope either. Story theory based on existing structures found in *completed* texts is of questionable value to writers who are keen to *create* an original story, not receive or analyse one. In addressing the full cycle of a story, it does not emerge in mind from a narration. The story begins in the mind of the author, *then becomes* a text and narration, and from there is rebuilt in the mind of the receiver. Syuzhet begets fabula for the receiver, but fabula (in the context of the author) begets the syuzhet in the first place; so structure is an inevitable *consequence* of creating a story, not a starting point for creation. As Syd Field (1979, pp.28-29) admits, "story determines structure", and yet all story theory based on long-established canonical story form (including Field's own 'dramatic principles' (ibid.) begins with a text and breaks it down into a structure which is handed back to aspiring writers as a mould into which story ideas should be shaped. This is a poor starting point, given that these advisors are writing guidance for writers of new stories, not for analysts of existing ones.

> Few screenplay manuals inspire confidence. If you want proof that contemporary Hollywood is formula-ridden, look no further than Syd Field's 'Paradigm.' (Bordwell, 2006, p.27)

Field's (1979) *Screenplay* was one of the first guides that "laid out the principles of dramatic structure" (Field, 1979, p.1) for film and television writers. Principles which define his "paradigm of dramatic structure" (ibid.) The setup is from page 1 to 30 of the script; confrontation runs from page 30 to 90 and the resolution from page 90 to 120 (Field, 1979, pp.21-30).

Field states that all good screenplays follow his paradigm, adding that the paradigm is "what holds the story together. It is the spine. The skeleton. Story determines structure; structure does not determine story" (Field, 1979, pp.28-29). However, this quotation is a contradiction in terms. Field directs his students to follow a set model, that is to develop their stories to fit a prescribed structure, and then argues that "story determines structure".

I argue that it is in Field's (1979) approach that the lacunae exist for all the story advice based on prescriptive structural imperatives. By deconstructing existing texts to develop structural imperatives for writers, structuralist theorists are beginning from the endpoint, the *outcome* of story creation, rather than beginning from the real starting point, the story idea and the writer's urge to communicate. If all good screenplays follow Field's 'paradigm', as he claims, it is because these canons have become institutionalised, and thereby perpetuated from one generation to the next, not because they are inevitable or archetypal.

Although Hollywood films generally do betray a slavish devotion to fulfil such principles, many of Field's absolutes are patently not true. For example, his assertion that 'all drama is conflict' (Field, 1979, p.25). The story of how two lovers met could include action, romance, character and story, and form a drama with minimal conflict, as exemplified by the film, *Amélie* (2001, directed by Jean-Pierre Jeunet). *La La Land* (2016, director Damien Chazelle) also largely fulfils this claim. Raymond Carver's story *Why Don't You Dance* (Carver, 2003) has no conflict, and is the basis for the Hollywood feature, *Everything Must Go* (directed by Dan Rush in 2011). The film of *Mary Poppins* (1964, directed by Robert Stevens) has minimal overarching conflict and no antagonist. Long periods and many sequences have little or no conflict, and yet the characters develop and drama is present. However, Field (1979), as with all the mainstream script advisors, insists that story cannot exist without conflict.

Over the decades, a circular argument developed. Film stories were made using the structural imperatives derived from canonical story form. Audiences learned to decode them. Analysts formalised them into a model. Gurus formalised them into 'How to Write' guidance for scriptwriters. Writers read the books and followed the model. The industry made money, so the business side began insisting that the model was followed. Film stories were made using the structural imperatives... It becomes very difficult to break, and very easy to justify and to perpetuate the circle.

Is there an alternative?

There have been many attempts to provide rule-based models that encompass every story. I am not aware of any that have not been foiled by stories coming to light that prove to be exceptions to the rules. I claim that by beginning with existing texts and breaking them down into common structural components, the analyst is starting from the wrong place; namely, the outcome of story creation. A great skeleton doth not a genius make, so I therefore propose a new starting point: the systems and modes of story creation.

Judgement of a story's 'quality' currently relies on the *invocation* of domain-based rules over the material objects in the domain (in this case, the formula-derived tick boxes asserted over a prospective film narrative). Macherey makes an important distinction here, because:

> ...a rigorous knowledge must beware of all forms of empiricism, for the objects of any rational investigation have no prior existence but are thought into being [...] The idea of a circle is not itself circular and does not depend on the existence of actual circles (Macherey, 1966, p.5-6.)

The theorist is searching for knowledge in the domain — the target material — and must effectively make up the answers, because, as we established earlier, there is no knowledge in the information world. Knowledge is only in mind. You may find circles in the real world, but knowledge of circles — 'the idea of a circle' — is not itself circular and is only in mind. Traditional structuralism is a realist investigation into what can be sensed, and knowledge cannot be sensed. To derive knowledge requires recognition of the phenomenological component. There is a clear difference between a circle in the real world and knowledge of circles, and what we are after in this investigation is the knowledge; the *meaning* of a circle. For that circle to have meaning, we must investigate this one and only circle in its given context (a knowledge context). If, for example, we make rules about all circles, then when we try to apply those rules to both a wedding ring and a roundabout, we find the rules are accurate... but not helpful. They are only observations on structure. It is one thing to identify a circle using science, mathematics, geometry — however, it is quite another to establish what a particular circle means. To get useful knowledge, we must investigate a specific circle and frame it with knowledge of its specific cultural context; a wedding ring or a roundabout in the context of human narrative and cultural meaning.

It is here that the traditional difficulty with structuralism lies. It's not possible to play squash without a wall, however there is no knowledge of squash in the wall. It is not possible to drink coffee without a receptacle but becoming a world expert on cups and mugs will reveal little of genuine value about coffee. It is not possible for a genius to exist without a skeleton, but the true substance of their genius is nothing to do with the skeleton.

In terms of this work, stories are researched on a similar, flawed basis. The structural imperatives applied to a text are like mugs, walls, skeletons and circles. They are of limited value, as there is no knowledge in a text. The structures that can be identified in a narration have little to do with knowledge of story — the phenomenological components within the content which provide the meaning. We can see if a story obeys the rules we attempt to invoke generally, but this is not going to give us knowledge of *this* story beyond its structure in the context of the system created by these syntagmatic rules.

> A knowledge of the work is not elaborated within the work, but supposes a distance between knowledge and its object (Macherey, 1966, pp. 84).

I assert that there can be no thorough scholarship undertaken in the study of story which ignores the author's creative process and the *knowledge* exchange necessary, between the author and the receiver, that gives it meaning. The knowledge exchange is surely the whole point of narration and to target this area to define narratology is to elevate our discipline beyond structuralism. No description of the conventions of textual structure can replace or explain the human behaviours, morals, ideology, learning, actions and interactions of characters in their story world. There is a human meaning that emerges from the knowledge embedded in the information stream, a human meaning which is not found in the structure of a text, and it is these knowledge dynamics that must form the basis of any narratological formalism if it is to, firstly, embrace story as well as narrative and, secondly, be useful.

At the root of his argument, Macherey highlights the differences between the denoted text and the 'illusion' created in mind through absorbing the text (an illusion which can also never be known or specified). Whilst the text is the only element which *can* be specified, in the sense that it is a material, tangible entity, it is not giving us meaning. It gives us information, however the meaning we receive is abstracted from that to an illusion in mind made from knowledge. A signifier (such as a rose) is not knowledge (there is no knowledge in nature) and is implicitly fictional when it is transmuted into a signification (love, courtship, romance). Similarly, a novel is mere information in itself and is explicitly fictional once interpreted.

> The work is a tissue of fictions: properly speaking it contains nothing that is true. However, in so far as it is not a total deception but a verified falsehood, it asks to be considered as speaking the truth: it is not just any old illusion, it is a determinate illusion (Macherey, 1966, p.69).

Even a true story is not the truth. The truth is gone, and the narration is a representation. However, even though it is fiction, a narration delivers material that becomes *meaning* in the mind of the receiver. There is no courtship or love in a flower. However, love and romance are the meaning within this fiction. Building meaning in mind from fiction is a puzzle that a receiver apparently seeks and enjoys.

Truth, lies and meaning

It is also important to make a distinction between truth and meaning. Truth is not useful to a narrative theory. If a narrative makes sense and has causal logic, it will be memorised and have meaning irrespective of any notion of 'truth'. A lie can create valid meaning just as readily. The narratives surrounding Santa Claus, for example, are just as meaningful as those surrounding a 'true' story and are laid down in mind just as readily. It is the presence of a complete narrative that triggers the mental processes of laying down a memory, not whether the narrative is true or not. It is in conscious memory that a user of narrative evaluates and situates a narrative for its value. The narratives surrounding Santa Claus may not be essential for putting food on the table or a roof over the family's head, but are valid and meaningful in the context of Christmas, holidays, religion, family bonding, happy children and so forth.

The great religions of the world are another interesting case in point. Let us say, for the sake of argument, that there are 100 religions in the world (I am not making any religious point here) and all are based on a book. A book of fables, allegories and moral stories that align the worshipers to a philosophy for running the community. These stories have great meaning that impacts the world. However, whilst the stories are not just the truth, they are the gospel truth that defines their lives, for other people — those who prefer a different religion or no religion — these stories are not any form of representative truth. They still have meaning, but no truth. So, meaning is there, because a religion can impact all of us, believers or not, however, truth is nebulous.

Although Macherey does use the word 'truth', I prefer to refer to *meaning* irrespective of any perceived truth. All story has meaning. We do not know if it has truth.

The receiver of a narration must decide on the meaning for them. That meaning is individual, and is not part of the work as presented:

> The book is not self-sufficient; it is necessarily accompanied by a certain absence, without which it would not exist. A knowledge of the book must include a consideration of this absence (Macherey, 1966, pp. 84,85).

Now we begin to see the definitive importance of the knowledge gap. It is precisely here — where knowledge is missing — that story exists. The meaning in the words of a story are, like the holes in a fishing net, a defining absence. The 'puzzle' in a story is in decoding all the significations, narrafications and storifications in order to find meaning that is indicated by the text but found in the mind of the receiver. The meaning is not present in the text. Meaning is built in mind through receiving and interpreting the text, bridging the gap between information and knowledge.

As the information is received by the senses and then interpreted into knowledge in mind, the gaps are bridged across the hermeneutic boundary to manifest as meaning created in mind by the receiver. The story is not the denoted information of the text; the story is built in mind, triggered by the text. I argue that the introduction of triggers for gap filling of this nature, from its simplest form (signifier -> signified) to the most complex of storifications is the core skill of the writer and that these gaps in knowledge are the substance of a story. A book is not a story. A film is not a story. A reader of a book or an audience member in a cinema is not a receiver of story. They are the receiver of narration, an interpreter of gaps and a producer of story.

The gaps in knowledge exist in mind, but are seeded in the text. It is the story in the author's mind that makes the text, and it is the triggers in the text that cause the story to be recreated in the mind of the receiver. The conditions that determine the production of the story in the mind of the receiver are a function of the determinate absences placed into the narration — the gaps between information and knowledge. As Macherey suggests:

> The work must be incomplete in itself: not extrinsically, in a fashion that could be completed to 'realise' the work. It must be emphasised that this incompleteness, betokened by the confrontation of separate meanings, is the true reason for its composition (Macherey, 1966, p.79).

This designed incompleteness in a text is the substance — or, more accurately, the *constitutive absence* of substance — that defines the presence of a story. The holes in a net are the constitutive absence that are the substance that defines the presence of a net. What is not there is absolutely critical to what we perceive and to what the net *means*. Story is a function of the dynamics and mechanisms of this constitutive absence — the absence of knowledge integral to information — that defines story. I argue through this work that the skill of the writer is in the crafting of knowledge gaps which constitute this absence and trigger the instinctive mental reflexes in the receiver. These mental reflexes are those fundamental mechanisms of mind that we identified earlier when we looked at how the mind works with signs and significations in real life.

I further argue that these constitutive absences are not merely an interesting relativist perspective. They are more than that. They are definitive and unavoidable. In the same way that it is not possible to have a signifier that makes sense without a signified, it is equally not possible to have a story that makes sense without gaps in knowledge. They are fundamental and define the substance of story. It is therefore an understanding of knowledge gaps of this nature that delivers an understanding of story. Knowledge gaps are fundamental, are present in both the information stream and in the meaning in mind, and may therefore be the common denominator for a narratology that is based not on information and structure, but upon knowledge and human nature.

3.2.1 Why Knowledge Gaps?

Let me explain with a practical example of how a paradigmatic analysis using knowledge gaps will work in comparison to an orthodox structuralist analysis of a film narration. Remember, a syntagmatic model starts with a rule base — in our case, the rules of the Hollywood formula — and *invokes* those rules from the outside in. A paradigmatic model *deduces* story characteristics from the inside out, in this case through identifying the key knowledge gaps within the specified text. Both methods use the same target film story, however, the former has its expectation pre-set by the demands of the Hollywood formula and the latter has only the method for analysis with no expectation.

The target film selected is *Some Like it Hot* (Wilder, 1959), and the aim is to establish the major dramatic dynamics which define the film story.

Orthodox analysis

The Hollywood formula applies domain-level rules (from the outside in), whereby the analyst must find an inciting incident that raises a key question in the mind of the audience during act 1 which remains open across the wide arc of the narration until, at climax, the question is answered. Applying this structuralist rule works fine and concludes that the inciting incident occurs when Joe (Tony Curtis) and Jerry (Jack Lemmon) witness a murder by the mob. They initially get away, but they have seen too much. The mob declares its ambition to track down and kill Joe and Jerry. The key question is raised: Will the mob find and kill Joe and Jerry, or will they escape? The question remains open across the wide arcs of the narration and is indeed answered at climax. The mob get involved with in-fighting, they contrive to kill each other and Joe and Jerry get away. From a structuralist perspective, based on the rule-base of the Hollywood formula, this is the main plot of *Some Like it Hot*.

Knowledge gap analysis

In contrast, analysis based upon identifying gaps in knowledge reveals that the longest, deepest and most persistent knowledge gap in *Some Like it Hot* is a subterfuge: Joe and Jerry are dressed as women and are hiding amongst women, living and behaving as women — Josephine and Daphne — in an all-girl band. The audience knows this, but no other participant does, so a knowledge gap is present between Joe and Jerry and all the other characters in the story world.

Because the knowledge gap approach derives its findings from the content of the narration and not from a rule-based approach applied generically to the domain of Hollywood movies, it inevitably draws from the characters, events and intent of the story. *Some Like it Hot* is primarily about two men who dress up as women and learn salutary lessons as they try to lead their lives as women. It is a story with themes and morality concerned with gender politics, the place of alternative gender constructions in society as experienced by two men dressed as women, and Sugar Kane — a real woman — all of which are implicit to the major knowledge gaps but which are missed in the primary findings of the structural approach.

> If we are to make sense of the concept of structure it must be with the recognition that structure is neither a property of the object nor a feature of its representation: the work does not derive from the unity of an intention which permeates it, nor from its conformity to an autonomous model (Macherey, 1966, p.40).

As we shall see shortly in the taxonomy of knowledge gaps, by focusing on the same mechanisms of mind described in section 1 — Narrative and Consciousness, there is a tendency to draw out the internal machinations of the characters and the story's 'meaning' rather than uncovering generalised structures through identifying turning points and conflict. I maintain that this is because the human meaning is derived from the gaps between the structures, so are precisely the elements that structuralism is unlikely to detect.

3.2.2   The Role of Structure

This does not mean that a structuralist approach is not valuable. Structure is an inevitable *consequence* of creating a story so an understanding of structure can be useful. However, because it is a consequence of creativity, structuralism provides a poor starting point for creation, and yet all story theory based on long-established canonical story form begins with a text and breaks it down into a structure, which is handed back to aspiring writers as a mould into which story ideas should be shaped. It is not surprising that structuralists begin with a text because influential work, such as that performed by critics, analysts, editors, agents, producers, directors and, of course, narratologists *do* begin with a text. These and many others *cannot begin their work* until they have a completed text. However, given that syntagmatic models such as the Hollywood formula are used to provide guidance for writers (who do *not* begin with a text), an existing narration is a poor starting point for creation. As Terry Eagleton points out:

> Having characterized the underlying rule-systems of a literary text, all the structuralist could do was sit back and wonder what to do next. There was no question of relating the work to the realities of which it treated, or to the conditions which produced it, or to the actual readers who studied it, since the founding gesture of structuralism had been to bracket off such realities (Eagleton, 2008, p.94-95).

Nowhere is this more true than with traditional story guidance. 'to bracket off' (ibid.) the mind and processes of the writer removes the possibility of analysing the creative processes that *generate* the text. By contrast, a theory of knowledge gaps *includes* and relies upon the process of the writer, because, as we have seen, knowledge gaps embedded by the writer's process become the implicit drivers of the writerly work of the receiver producing the story in mind. The discipline of analysis thereby increases its scope. Instead of capturing the dynamics between a text and its receiver, it makes a subtle shift towards the knowledge exchange between writer and receiver. However, there is surely a structure involved in the mediation, so can it not also be useful and included? Yes, it can. We must not forget that structure is inevitable. The text:

> is not independent, but bears in its material substance the imprint of a determinate absence which is also the principle of its identity. [...] It is not a question of perceiving a latent structure of which the manifest work is an index, but of establishing that absence around which a real complexity is knit (Macherey, 1966, p.80, 101).

If the writer process is viewed as a matter of creating and embedding knowledge gaps, then knowledge gaps can be seen to be fundamental to the structure that will be an inevitable consequence of creating the text. While it is true to say that a fishing net is made of string and the string tells us where the holes are, it is equally true to say that the holes in a fishing net tell us where the string is. A fishing net is made of holes. A story is made of gaps in knowledge. A story is a constitutive absence of knowledge. If we know where the holes are we know the structure. The answer then is surely to apply structuralism to the knowledge gaps themselves; to establish the language of (the system of) knowledge gaps (the subject of section 4), and because the holes are filled by subtext provided by the receiver, the structure that is revealed will be directly associated with the 'emotional' content that composes the story — that derived from character behaviours, decisions and interactions.

Thus, in the scope of the 'language of' knowledge gaps, we begin with the story creator and their process of production. An author begins with a blank page (a single, enormous, all-encompassing knowledge gap) and breaks that down into a large number of constitutive gaps that, through the boundaries that define the gaps, implicitly prescribe the associated structure (a structure defined through the system of knowledge gaps). These gaps are present and tangible in the text the author produces so are available to be measured under analysis.

The Moment of Conversion

An author does not push their story into the receiver; a receiver senses the gaps and *draws the story out of themselves*. A great story is made of cues and pointers to those knowledge gaps that invite the receiver to populate the gap with knowledge they already have (or can logically deduce or infer) from their own history and experience. When a writer leaves a knowledge gap in their work, the reader is compelled to be writerly. The reader will sense the gap, which will trigger their engagement, they will project knowledge into the gap, and this will give them a sense of ownership and involvement. The story becomes part of them, because they are producing much of it for themselves by filling in the knowledge gaps crafted into place by the author.

Let's take an example of what a knowledge gap is and how it works using a short extract from the Brothers Grimm version of *Little Red Riding Hood*. Remember, the denoted information — objective information that provides factual, unambiguous material needing minimal interpretation — provides the structural framework for the story. The connotative knowledge is that which we, as readers, derive for ourselves by projecting into the gaps; the constitutive absence of knowledge lying in the gaps between the denoted information. First, then, the extract:

> Little Red Riding Hood skipped happily on her way to visit her sick grandmother. The grandmother lived out in the wood, half a league from the village, and just as Little Red Riding Hood entered the wood, a wolf met her. Red Riding Hood did not know what a wicked creature he was, and was not at all afraid of him.
>
> 'Good day, Little Red Riding Hood,' said he.
>
> 'Thank you kindly, wolf.'
>
> 'Whither away so early, Little Red Riding Hood?'
>
> 'To my grandmother's.'
>
> 'What have you got in your apron?'
>
> 'Yesterday was baking-day, so poor sick grandmother is to have something good, to make her stronger.'
>
> 'Where does your grandmother live, Little Red Riding Hood?'
>
> 'A good quarter of a league farther on in the wood; her house stands under the three large oak-trees, the nut-trees are just below; you surely must know it,' replied Little Red Riding Hood.
>
> So he walked for a short time by the side of Little Red Riding Hood, and then he said: 'See, Little Red Riding Hood, how pretty the flowers are about here - why do you not look round? I believe, too, that you do not hear how sweetly the little birds are singing; you walk gravely along as if you were going to school, while everything else out here in the wood is merry.'
>
> Little Red Riding Hood raised her eyes, and when she saw the sunbeams dancing here and there through the trees, and pretty flowers growing everywhere, she thought: 'Suppose I take grandmother a fresh nosegay; that would please her too. It is so early in the day that I shall still get there in good time.'
>
> So she ran from the path into the wood to look for flowers. And whenever she had picked one, she fancied that she saw a still prettier one farther on, and ran after it, and so got deeper and deeper into the wood.

> Meanwhile the wolf ran straight to the grandmother's house and knocked at the door.
>
> 'Who is there?'
>
> 'Little Red Riding Hood,' replied the wolf. 'Bringing cake and wine; open the door.'
>
> 'Lift the latch,' called out the grandmother, 'I am too weak, and cannot get up.'
>
> The wolf lifted the latch, the door sprang open, and without saying a word he went straight to the grandmother's bed, and devoured her. Then he put on her clothes, dressed himself in her cap, laid himself in bed and drew the curtains.

In order to analyse these words in knowledge gap terms, I am going to have to suggest possible author and receiver activities. Please accept that these suggestions are provided in order to exemplify the paradigmatic characteristics of the methodology. It is acknowledged that these suggestions are purely speculative, and at no point am I claiming to 'know' the mindset of the author or receiver. However, what I can specify is the presence of a knowledge gap which, I claim, acts as a trigger on the receiver. The trigger is unconscious and automatic, and gap filling is inevitable given a capable receiver. However, I fully acknowledge that the nature of the receiver response cannot be specified. A suggestion for a possible response is made for the purposes of exemplification.

Firstly, then, there is denoted information. For example:

> Red Riding Hood did not know what a wicked creature he was, and was not at all afraid of him.

This denoted information causes a capable receiver to draw on their own experience to connotate the knowledge that the narrative is tempting us to build in. We see the contrast between the wolf's wickedness and Red Riding Hood's naivety and we begin to 'produce' story in mind over and above the given text. The denoted framework causes us to project into the gap; that Red Riding Hood is vulnerable in the context of the wolf. In life, when we sense a knowledge gap we sense risk and opportunity, and these are surely represented by Little Red Riding Hood (risk) and the wolf (opportunity) in this sentence. The author is encouraging us to project ahead; this story is likely to feature the wolf's wickedness progressing successfully in the light of Red Riding Hood's naivety.

Similarly:

> So she ran from the path into the wood to look for flowers. And whenever she had picked one, she fancied that she saw a still prettier one farther on, and ran after it, and so got deeper and deeper into the wood.

This is denoted text. No ambiguity. However, our knowledge of wolves and naivety has us projecting into the implied gap once more. We fear that Red Riding Hood is distracted; her dalliance with the flowers is going to be her downfall. Why does this work? Because there is a knowledge gap between what the wolf intends and what Red Riding Hood knows. As readers, we realise that the wolf has a plan, and a character plan has three implicit gaps: firstly, between those who know of the plan (wolf) and those who do not (Red Riding Hood). Secondly, in the question that is raised: Will the plan succeed? And thirdly, in the gap between the plan and the way it is playing out in the character's world. We in the audience are fully cognisant of these gaps between our knowledge and Little Red Riding Hood's lack of knowledge. This is the basis of the story's fundamental power to grip and engage.

> The wolf put on Grandmother's clothes, dressed himself in her cap, laid himself in bed and drew the curtains.

The writer erects denoted struts which point their readers towards the knowledge gaps. The connotation will take place in the mind of the reader in the space between the framework denotations. As receivers, we cannot help it. The cognitive map we are building naturally demands a narrative structure, so it accepts the denoted information and projects human causal logic from personal knowledge and experience to construct a story. Given the actions and motivation of the wolf and the naivety of Little Red Riding Hood, we can readily project a story forwards in which the wolf will trick, trap and eat the little girl. Our emotions are aroused, because when we project knowledge into the gaps in the developing narrative logic, we see danger for the girl. We read that Little Red Riding Hood 'skipped happily', but we feel she should not be happy. We want to educate her against her naivety. We read that the wolf is dressed as a grandmother. A disguise is a knowledge gap between the presented identity (a grandmother) and the hidden identity (a wolf). However, our instinct to project the narrative forwards, with innate story logic — even when we were aged four — only sees the awful implications for Little Red Riding Hood. We are projecting ahead and receiving the real story — the one we are drawing out of ourselves — by introducing new material that is connotated and projected into the gaps; the subtext.

An orthodox deconstruction of *Little Red Riding Hood* will look for an inciting incident to raise a key question, and it finds it: Will the wolf trap and eat Red Riding Hood? And the question is answered at climax. This is also a knowledge gap; the gap between the question and its answer, so this orthodox structuralist element is also captured by a knowledge gap paradigm. As we shall see in the taxonomy, it turns out that all the most common structural imperatives have a knowledge gap representation. Whilst I argue that the knowledge gap perspective is better connected to the characters and content of the story, knowledge gaps also capture the orthodox structures. This means that a movement towards knowledge gaps does not throw out the baby with the bathwater. Valid structures are captured in the language of knowledge gaps, but as part of a wider scope than a traditional structural model, because it includes the writer, the text, the narration and the receiver.

Where an orthodox analysis of Little Red Riding Hood would identify the key question (Will the wolf trap and eat Little Red Riding Hood?), it stops there with the black/white, yes/no answer. It would not recognise it as being part of a plan, or connect the key question with the inherent character motivations and weaknesses (naivety and wickedness) that are present in the knowledge gaps. Additionally, the traditional approach is defeated by the twist at climax. Red Riding Hood is rescued by the woodcutter, and the wolf is killed, so although the answer to the key question was 'yes' (the wolf did trap and eat Red Riding Hood) she ended up winning out. The knowledge gap approach does not 'major' on the key question — this is just another knowledge gap — while the deeper, more pervasive knowledge gaps are in the motivations and morality of the story — so the knowledge gap approach captures the essence of the story more closely and perceptively. Why? Because, as we established earlier, a story is not a matter of fact or fiction. It is a matter of text and subtext. The text is a form of structural truth, but the subtext is a form of meaning. As discussed earlier, the truth is not useful or reliable or even present, but meaning is key and meaning is always there. The truth is rarely in the text but the meaning is always in the subtext. Orthodox analysis captures a truth about structure. Knowledge gaps capture subtext and meaning. Indeed, knowledge gaps have a direct, one-to-one relationship with subtext, so let us go more deeply into this critical word.

3.2.3 Subtext

The term 'subtext' entered the English language relatively recently, in the 1950s, in a translation of Konstantin Stanislavski's book, *An Actor Prepares* (1936). The term never featured in the proliferation of guidance for writers through the main wave of development of the film industry in the Western world. The topic of subtext is therefore not well explored, yet in most contemporary guidance it is stated that stories should be delivered in subtext.

In common usage, we understand subtext to mean 'what lies beneath'. When we see the sea whilst watching *Jaws* (1975, directed by Steven Spielberg) — or even just hear that iconic musical theme — we sense a shark even though we cannot see one. Subtext can also refer to the unstated messages in a story, such as the moral message in a children's story, the allegory in a Bible story, or the ideological message within a novel (such as the implicit criticism of Communism implied in George Orwell's *Animal Farm* [1945]). There is a gap between what is given and what is received, and the knowledge that goes into that gap is the subtext. What is given is the sea, what we receive is a shark. The material the receiver provides to the production in mind through their own writerly work is the subtext.

A story comprises knowledge derived from the denoted content of the information stream plus the knowledge drawn from the receiver's own existing knowledge in mind. The latter is the subtext; the knowledge that goes into a gap. If you think about the dynamics involved in your reception of the Hemingway short story ("For Sale. Children's Shoes. Never Worn"), the majority of the knowledge that makes up the final story in your mind comes from within yourself. Some knowledge comes from the denoted information, but the story mostly comes from your own cultural knowledge and experience 'activated' into existence through interpretation of the denoted information and the drive to fill the gaps. You may perceive that the Hemingway text is a classified advertisement and question yourself: Why is this person selling children's shoes that have not been worn? Why have the shoes not been worn? By answering these questions in your own mind, you filled the gaps (with the subtext) and created the story for yourself.

I argue that this dynamic defines story, because subtext is a component of all stories. A narration is made from text, comprising signifiers and signifieds. However, a complete story is made from signs, significations, narrafications and storification, and it is the subtext drawn from the receiver's knowledge and experience that elevates the signified into signification and the narrafications into storifications. As pointed out earlier, an author does not push a story into you, they give you a narration, and you draw their story out of yourself. Subtext is the generic term for the knowledge that is brought from personal knowledge and experience to fill the knowledge gaps.

Strictly speaking, a narrative instantly becomes a story the moment it is held in working memory. 'The cat sat on the mat' is a story as soon as it is held in mind. However, this story is a simplistic representation of the denoted narrative, with only the subtext required to accurately derive signifieds from signifiers. From here, it is a sliding scale of writerly work to the point of storification, where the final story in mind is significantly different from, and/or greater than, the denoted material that inspired it ('For Sale. Baby's Shoes. Never Worn'), and it requires a great deal more subtext to be provided by the writerly work of the receiver.

The difference in story complexity is in the demands placed on the receiver in terms of the writerly work required or, to put it another way, the quantity of subtext that goes in to completing it. In researching the knowledge gap profiles of many stories, there appears to be a correlation between the public rating of a story and the amount of subtext it contains. The more subtext there is (the more writerly work done, the more knowledge gaps there are...), the higher the story is rated.

Writers craft the knowledge potential in such a way as to coax the reader to fill the knowledge gap with the subtext the writer desires them to bring to the story. The writer of *Little Red Riding Hood* did not tell us that the wolf was waiting to pounce on Little Red Riding Hood and eat her. The writer said the wolf: '...put on her [Grandma's] clothes, dressed himself in her cap, laid himself in bed and drew the curtains.'

We made our own assumptions from this, because of our understanding of wolves and their motivation. This is a fine example of a writer creating the conditions for subtext, by using denoted information to create a gap; a gap between an action within a narrative and the expected logical outcome of that narrative progression (the human logical reason why the wolf might be running this script). By creating this gap and inviting such projection, the story requires writerly work, is therefore delivered in subtext and is thereby imbued with the dynamics that trigger engagement. A knowledge gap is the trigger that causes a receiver to generate subtext.

Knowledge gaps are the absence which constitutes the story. Subtext is the material that goes into the gaps. Once gaps are open and the subtext required is not yet clear, the evolutionary mental reflexes discussed in section 1 have been triggered and the receiver is likely to remain engaged until the gaps are filled. As with the example of the bump in the night, the receiver cannot just forget it, move on and do something else. The story has done to their brain what nature does in real life. Knowledge gaps alert us to risk or opportunity, and the story thereby has a visceral grip. It is not that the receiver is in danger themselves — they are receiving a narration — but the way the narration is constructed triggers those same instinctive reactions which important events trigger in real life.

An author will continuously open, protract and pay-off knowledge gaps, but that is not all. If the ongoing delivery of the story means that the cognitive map becomes completed using storifications, it will transcend the obvious connotations. The storification in *Little Red Riding Hood* is a moral message and the whole story will teach the receiver a lesson about human life such that the four-year-old receiving *Little Red Riding Hood* may leave the story with the belief that it is unwise to talk to strangers. This message is not denoted in the text but is connotated by the child through their writerly work. From my analysis of the knowledge gap profiles of the most highly rated stories, it seems that the stories we appreciate the most are the ones with the finest storifications. A brain craves knowledge — it is our evolutionary advantage. If a story delivers a reader a lesson about life and how it should be led, or resonates with a sagely moral imperative, it seems that story will be more popular with its audience. The power in *Little Red Riding Hood* — how it is delivered and the gaps it opens and then invites us to fill — is why it has sustained an audience — and taught children a life lesson — for close to 1000 years (for a history of the story, see Thurston-Joy, 2003).

However, returning to our earlier theme, a writer has to be careful. Each reading is an individual production of a story, and the writer wants to provide gaps in knowledge into which their intended audience will consistently project in similar ways, otherwise they will receive different or confused stories. This is the art of writing that differentiates the finest stories. By providing a denoted story framework, and enough cues towards the gaps in knowledge, all competent receivers of the story will complete their mental narrative in similar enough ways to receive broadly the same story, despite having constructed much of it for themselves. This is masterful story delivery through the expert use of knowledge gaps.

The more ambiguous and wider the knowledge gaps, the more likelihood there is of multiple interpretations or even confusion. However, knowledge gaps with a plurality of potential interpretations also characterise the most lauded of stories. Shakespeare and poetry, for example, have knowledge gaps that cause ongoing interpretation and analysis by experts for centuries, they polarise opinion, and yet the extra work the audience must do to create the story in mind sees them find a greater depth of appreciation and engagement from their efforts. In opera, the story is highly abstracted from the denoted material we are given, and what words there are may be delivered in Latin, and yet the emotion inspired by the story can be extraordinary.

To summarise, the hermeneutic boundary is the point at which information is interpreted into knowledge. In story terms, that is interpretation of the actions, experiences and decisions of the actors and the consequential outcomes. However, if the story created in mind has gaps in it, the receiver will provide the missing knowledge (the subtext) to complete the story for themselves. The story is then coming from two places: the denoted material of the narration, and the connotated contribution from the knowledge and experience of the receiver. Note how, in this summary, the dynamics of the story are not defined by the structure of the text. The text can be bracketed off as a conduit, merely facilitating the communication between the author and receiver. The story dynamics of interest are in the knowledge exchange between the author (and the gaps they leave) and the receiver (and the gaps they fill).

3.3 Truth and Fiction

Homo sapiens is a relatively weak physical specimen. We rely on intellect to keep safe, so have evolved an instinctive and highly tuned aversion to a perceived lack of knowledge. As the saying goes, 'knowledge is power' (Bacon, 1597), so gaps in our knowledge in the real world arouse us because they are indicators of risk. If we don't have solid facts with which to fill a knowledge gap, we project knowledge into the gap and we will act on the best fit narrative we can create that gives it logical completeness. How do we know, when we create a narrative and rely on it in this way, if we have created a form of truth (or as I would rather express it, a 'reliable meaning') that will narrate us to safety and prosperity or a flawed meaning that may lead to a fall?

In the modern age, our lives are so insulated from danger and from our natural enemies that our judgement in these terms is rarely tested to extremes. However, because our evolutionary selves still predominate in our mental drives, our brains still function in the same atavistic ways they did when we were barely upright. This is why stories are so intuitively engaging.

To bring stories and evolutionary drives closer still, it is important to recognise that a memory of a real-world event is not the truth. Even if memories are created from direct, real-world experience they are still only a *representation* of the truth, held in mind. The truth is gone from the moment the actual event is over. A witness or participant's memory is the closest thing we have to that truth after the event, but it has been filtered through the lens of human senses into human logic. Further still, the only way a witness can communicate that event to another is through the limiting lens language and interpretation. We equate fiction with falsehood. We equate nonfiction with truth. However, the process of internalising an event fictionalises it. The mental narrative version of an event is a human-sanitised interpretation of that event, not the truth.

Thus we either have memories and learning laid down by experiencing an event OR we have memories and learning laid down by having an event communicated to us. Both end up as representations in mind. As an example of how we remember 'truth', think about what happens when one reads a book. A reader does not memorise the words and sentences that make up the textual 'truth'. A reader commits to memory a phenomenological representation of the causal logic.

> Readers tend to remember the mental model they constructed from a text rather than the text itself (Bower and Morrow, 1990, p.44).

You remember the story of *Little Red Riding Hood*, but you do not remember the words that composed that story. To whatever extent the words of a narrative are an attempt to represent truth, the receiver assimilates them into a phenomenological representation that is another abstracted version. The same is true of all narrative. The story created in mind by the receiver can never be the same as the author's vision, and nobody can ever know how close the interpreted world-in-mind is to the original vision, because the writerly work done by the receiver will render it unique to every interpretation; and the author is not there to tell us their 'truth'. Even if the author was there to recall their 'truth', the author's recollected truth would not be the truth. Memory is bent by time and experience, and is only memory — a representation of remembered 'truth', even for the author.

> We create our memories even as they create us—a Möbius strip, an Escher print, a double helix, if you will, from which the blueprint of self emerges. It's both dazzling and chilling to realize that the narrative arc of our lives relies on a phenomenon that is by turns robust, fallible, malleable, potent, slippery, inventive, and above all, powerfully yoked to emotion. (Neimark, 2004, p.77)

How can this fallibility, this designed falsehood, serve us well? The reason is that we value the human meaning in an event far more than we feel any need to remember the truth. As Neimark suggests in her investigation into the memories of people who believe they have been abducted by aliens, meaning trumps truth every time (ibid.). Our instinctive drive is not simply to fill in knowledge gaps to create a story, but to create a story *out of* human values. To create a narrative-in-mind that equips us to do better in our own lives. We are humans in a natural world, so our drive is not to promote and enhance the natural world, but to promote and enhance our human prospect. (Pursuing this aim with these priorities even, apparently, to the ultimate destruction of the natural world that sustains us!) The more resonant the narrative is to *human* values, the more kudos it carries and the more memorable it becomes.

Within the broader human and perhaps moral context, the receiver will also personalise. They can only interpret a text in terms of themselves; an interpretation shaped by personality, age, gender, conditioning, prevailing culture, intelligence, life experience, values and their 'competence' to interpret. Even a re-reading of a text by the same reader will be experienced differently from previous readings on the basis of fore-knowledge of the story and simple things such as their mood at the time of reading or changes in life experience, age, values and so on.

Note, then, that even with a narration that comprises denoted truth, the interpretive process will skew that truth to accommodate the mindset of the receiver. The writerly work they do will overlay their own production values, firstly in the context of human evolutionary drives, and secondly in the context of their personal conditioning, biases, knowledge and experience.

The Chicken or the Egg?

Given that linguistics is part of basic animal communication, but sophisticated communication arrived long after human existence, which came first — the script or the narrative? Do we think in language? Since people first recognised the power of storytelling as a means of affecting a mind, theorists have been looking at it in that direction, asking: Why are stories so powerful? What is the story impact on the human mind? What is it about the structure of a good story that makes it grip and engage? Theorists begin from an existing text and analyse it for structures and universals in search of the drivers for the compulsion to gestalt that appears to be loaded into both the human receiver and the essence of a narration. The implication being that the brain takes a narrative from the real world and thinks, 'Hmm, that's a great way to remember things. I'll use story dynamics to organise my memories from now on.' Of course, the reality is the other way around. A text could not be analysed by a mind until a story had been produced by a mind. The mind came first, the text came later.

Mikhail Bakhtin stated that "there can be no human consciousness without a system of signs," (Bakhtin, 1928; p.102), which gives pause for thought. We think that language comes out of us, because we talk it and use it continuously to explain ourselves and express our ideas. But language is not a product of the person; it is more true to say that a person is a product of the language. Language creates a society of aligned individuals. In the modern developmental sense, language is there before we are born, we grow into it and it educates us with the pre-sets laid down by millennia of previous generations. Language allows us to express ourselves and unites us.

However, language also comes into us as we grow; limits and constrains us and makes us reliant upon constructed significations and communicated myth. Despite its sophistication and wonder, language is a reductive tool, capturing only a small percentage of an entire experienced event; the rest of the event being a constitutive absence that the receiver of language must fill if they are to be empowered by a complete script that makes human causal logical sense and brings understood benefit. So, even language itself is a function of knowledge gaps. We fill a gap every time we learn a new word (contextualise a new signifier) and every time we interpret it into a meaning-in-mind (signified). We fill a more sophisticated gap each time we empty a signified by interpreting it through the lens of cultural experience and fill it with signification. We add still further gaps every time we interpret groups of signifieds joined into meta-meanings, and further again through narrafication. Yes, we think in language, however, when language was simple, we were simple. Dog language is simple, and dogs are simple. Language is the key to ascension on to the intellectual plane of shared human consciousness, and we do this by filling knowledge gaps (or 'learning'). Language creates the individuals and the communities, societies and ideologies they build. When we think about evolution, we think about the more physical, experiential side; however, because the intellectual, linguistic plane is there before we are born, the process of being formed out of the same language as each other renders us fundamentally the same as each other. Language and narrative are the keys to learning and joining the intellectual plane.

I argue that the brain stores memories in the way it always has done. Narrative maps created from experience, scripts and imagination; the instinctive mechanisms of mind which were there before language, and it was these mental dynamics that shaped language when it eventually came along. The mind and its narrative dynamics were there first, so when language and narration arrived it was only natural that they would emerge in a structure and form derived from the way our mind was already working in the first place. The first question is not: 'What is the story impact on mind?' What theorists should be asking is: 'What is the process of mind which can help us to understand why it produces stories?'

I argue that the process of mind is the process of narrative construction, identification and manipulation. Intelligence is a function of a huge number of scripts, all structured as narratives, pre-set by evolution and honed by education and experience into expectations for how events will pan out in the face of our actions. We rely on the accuracy of the expectations and we act upon them. When events do not match expectation, we activate our intellect and project into the gaps, but we are always seeking a narrative that will logically bring us understanding of our situation in the world and take us to a desired outcome.

When we have to fill in knowledge gaps to learn something, we learn that lesson thoroughly and, as we have seen, we may embed narrative memories we subsequently use in our lives going forwards. This makes communication through knowledge gaps an extremely powerful tool; the most powerful tool of teaching and learning outside of direct personal experience. And what do we call this type of communication?

Stories.

**A reader is not simply a consumer of text, but a producer of story.
Every reading of a story is a unique production of that story.**

1.1.1   A story definition

One of the things that surprised me most when I first began research in narratology is that the term 'story' has never been satisfactorily defined. Since Aristotle more than 2,300 years ago, nobody has ever come up with a definition that has satisfied all authorities and which covers everything most people would all intuitively agree to be a 'story'.

Given my epistemological assumptions, at its most simplistic, the following definition captures every story:

A story is a narrative in mind.

It is stimulated from information in the outside world and constructed through interpreting the information into mind and then contextualising it into human sense using knowledge from the receiver's own experience. In fiction terms, it is a joint effort between an author and a receiver. The problems with definition come when we attempt to differentiate between a 'good' story and a 'bad' story, which of course is subjective. Qualitative evaluation is often a matter of surveys and statistically compelling agreement across large numbers of respondents. What can be said with a degree of confidence from my research is that the more knowledge gaps there are, the deeper they run and the longer they persist, the higher the story is rated by public review. In other words, although a story with fewer, lesser gaps is still a story ('the cat sat on the mat'), those with more complex gaps (significations, narrafications and storifications) require more writerly work and are, it would seem, more satisfying for the receiver. In addressing the 'causes' of story and the perceived quality of a story, it is reasonable to say that, because knowledge gaps have their part to play at every level of linguistic formation (signs, signification, narrafication and storification), it can be said that:

A story is inspired into mind by any form of communication that includes knowledge gaps in the telling.

Without going into deeply subjective waters, we can say that knowledge gaps arise from our evolutionary psychology and are fundamental to the formation of narrative in mind and therefore to the presence of story. What can be said then about knowledge gaps? How many types of knowledge gaps are there? Which knowledge gaps are the most powerful? How can we understand them? How can we use this to inform narratology?

3.3.1 Knowledge gaps

In any narration, a knowledge gap is said to exist whenever there is a difference in the knowledge held between any of the participants. Within the context of this definition, a 'participant' is any entity that is capable of holding (or withholding) knowledge, such as:

- A character
- The receiver (the audience, spectator, viewer, reader)
- The author
- The narrator
- Extra-textual information (such as paratext)
- Impactful third parties or objects
- Events.

A safe withholds information and, therefore, can be a component of a knowledge gap. A playing card face down on a poker table in the wild west withholds knowledge capable of causing bedlam and death when revealed in a saloon bar. A film's poster or trailer presents information but simultaneously withholds knowledge and intrigues a receiver. A deluded man embodies a knowledge gap between his self-image and his own reality. A character's plan contains several gaps in knowledge, for example in the question: Will the plan succeed? And in the difference in the knowledge held by those who know about the plan and those who do not. A line of dialogue can both give knowledge and withhold it at the same time (for example, a lie). A wrapped present. (Is there any more wonderful example of the power of withheld information than a wrapped present?!) Any action, object or character that can hold or withhold information can generate a knowledge gap if the knowledge held is not equal across all participants in the story.

If we are to create a language of knowledge gaps that can be used as a common denominator for comparative analysis, we must understand how they operate. The following section is given over to creating a complete taxonomy of knowledge gaps.

4 A Taxonomy of Knowledge Gaps

> **As we know, there are known knowns; there are things we know we know. We also know there are known unknowns; that is to say we know there are some things we do not know. But there are also unknown unknowns – the ones we don't know we don't know.**
>
> **Donald Rumsfeld, US Defence Secretary (2002)**

Knowledge gaps are a definitive substance (the constitutive absence) of story. As they are a function of the knowledge domain, they exist only in mind. However, the potential to grow that gap in the mind is sourced from the material in the narration, so knowledge gaps must also be a function of the information domain. Further, as all semiotic systems are finite sets, there should be a closed set of knowledge gaps. It should be possible to find the sources of knowledge gaps seeded in the information stream, identify them, document them and understand how they work. If there are tangible, countable elements in the information stream, this further implies that every story can be comprehensively quantified by its knowledge gaps. It may further be asserted that once stories are quantified in the same way, with knowledge gaps as the common denominator, the knowledge gap profile of a story will be a unique 'fingerprint' of that individual story and will have characteristics that will be revealing in comparison to the knowledge gap profiles of other stories.

In my research I selected four case studies (Hollywood films from across the 20th century) and set about apprehending as many knowledge gaps as I could find in the target film stories. I went through each film story moment by moment, pausing at regular intervals, and whenever there was a difference in the knowledge held by two participants, I noted it down, and, as patterns emerged, I began grouping them. The result is the taxonomy documented in this chapter, with an explanation of each type, class and category.

Three points to note:

- Hollywood film has primarily been used in the case studies and examples, however a knowledge gap approach is independent of the medium. The taxonomy of knowledge gaps is applicable to all stories in all media. There will certainly be some gaps which are possible in one media but not in another, but as far as practicable, this taxonomy is media independent and applicable to all stories in any medium.
- If you are a writer, a more focussed and somewhat reduced version of this taxonomy, selected specifically to be useful to writers, is at the core of my more practical work: *The Primary Colours of Story* (Baboulene, 2019). If you are looking for applied value from this research, the version of this taxonomy in the commercial work is tailored for you.
- The four films used as my case studies are:

FILM STORY	DIRECTOR	YEAR
MODERN TIMES	CHARLIE CHAPLIN	1936 UNITED ARTISTS
THE BIG SLEEP	HOWARD HAWKS	1946 WARNER BROTHERS
SOME LIKE IT HOT	BILLY WILDER	1959 UNITED ARTISTS
BACK TO THE FUTURE	ROBERT ZEMEKIS	1985 UNIVERSAL

Whilst the four films are not discussed equally in this work, the findings come from across them all (and many others informally). A broader discussion, including complete case studies for all four target films, can be found in my doctoral thesis: *Knowledge Gaps in Popular Hollywood Cinema: The role of information disparity in film narrative* (Baboulene, 2017), available as an eBook through online retail outlets.

4.1 Rationale

Modern Times (1936, dir. Charles Chaplin) was chosen for analysis because it is representative of early Hollywood and the silent era (although sound does feature in the film) and it is made by one of the world's greatest stars and most recognised characters. Whereas most films are highly collaborative and represent a mélange of input, egos and opinions, the comparative autonomy of Charlie Chaplin, the historical context of his film-making as well as his well-documented personal history renders *Modern Times* a relatively accessible example of a film with a social subtext, addressing the prevailing socio-economic situation in the USA at the time and the auteur's feelings about it. It is also a film story with an unorthodox structure in the context of classical Hollywood style, being a series of 'episodes', each a comic set-piece rather than a singular story told across a wide arc defined by a key question.

The Big Sleep (1946, directed by Howard Hawks) was selected for analysis because the star images and off-screen relationships of Hawks, Lauren Bacall and Humphrey Bogart form part of the narration that creates knowledge gaps outside of the diegesis; the film noir credentials facilitate an investigation of genre; it is a mystery story (the only one in the case studies); and it is an example of the studio system at the peak of its operation in the 1940s. Above all, it has a notoriously confusing plot, rendering it an interesting narratological paradox, given that it is such a highly rated film story.

Some Like it Hot (1959, directed by Billy Wilder) is of significance to this research because of the time in which it was made (towards the end of the Classical Hollywood period); the resonance of Marilyn Monroe at the height of her fame, facilitating a discussion of star image; and the significance of the gender dynamics as both a factor in cinema politics and an example of the way knowledge gaps relate to the content of a narrative in ways that distinguish it from a structural analysis.

Back to the Future (1985, directed by Robert Zemeckis) was selected for analysis as it is one of a number of films that heralded a successful renaissance of the Classical Hollywood approach to film-making. It is also an example of a film narration structured in the classical style recommended by the structural imperatives of the contemporary Hollywood film script gurus discussed in section 2. That is, it is a definitive example of the Hollywood formula.

In order to create a usable paradigm, we must understand what it is we are searching for inside a specific story. The answer is 'gaps in knowledge between different participants in the narration'. The next job, then, is to analyse the set of target narrations and build up a taxonomy of knowledge gaps.

4.2 Knowledge Gap Taxonomy

The table below provides an overview, followed by an explanation of each of the classifications, categories and types.

Table 1 - Knowledge Gap Taxonomy Overview

	TAXONOMY OF KNOWLEDGE GAPS				
CLASS	All knowledge gaps are either **PRIVILEGE or REVELATION**				
	All knowledge gaps are either **SIMPLE, COMPOUND or COMPLEX**				
CATEGORY	**PARATEXT**	**DIEGESIS**			**STORIFY**
		DIEGETIC ORIENTING TEXT	MIMETIC ORIENTING TEXT	MIMETIC TEXT	
TYPE	Star Image Character Image Marketing and Promo' Material	Self-Conscious Narrator Promise Sound/Light Story World Ellipsis Gaps	Key questions Event questions Character Plans Motivation Conflict Harmatia Education Backstory	Hermeneutic Questions Subterfuge Subplot Action/Dialogue Suggestion/Implication Suspense Misdirection/Mis-interpretation Comedy Distraction Mise-en-scène Anagnorisis	Surpassing Aims Character Growth Education Vicarious Learning The Moral Argument Peripeteia Metaphor/Allegory Recognition/Allusion

4.3 Classifications

All knowledge gaps are classified as either **privilege** or **revelation**, and either **simple, compound or complex**.

4.3.1 Privilege and Revelation

All knowledge gaps involve a difference in the knowledge held by two participants, such as the narrator, a character or the receiver of the narration (audience, spectator, listener…). The implication is that there are two sets of participants: the informed or the knowing, who have knowledge others do not have; and the uninformed or unknowing who lack knowledge held by others. These dynamics change continuously as the narration progresses. For example, before the narration commences, the author knows everything and the receiver knows nothing, and this difference reduces as knowledge is conveyed.

For the purposes of classification, a single perspective has been adopted relative to the receiver of the narration, because, without a receiver, there is no human meaning to the narrative and there is no story. The presence of the gap is a function of the receiver, who will either know more or less than another participant. For this reason, labels are assigned to these two dynamics: the receiver will always experience a knowledge gap as either **privilege** knowledge (information they have, but which at least one other participant does not) or **revelation** knowledge (information that at least one other participant has, but which the receiver does not).

4.3.1.1 Revelation Gaps

A revelation gap involves the receiver being denied knowledge that is held by at least one other participant. This is a recognised mechanism in narrative delivery. Tomashevsky (1925, pp.63-80) termed this "delayed exposition" and presented it as a method for building tension.

At the climax of *Back to the Future*, Marty McFly (Michael J. Fox) returns to 1985 from his time-travel adventure to 1955 and is distraught to find he has got back too late to prevent his friend Doc Brown (Christopher Lloyd) from being gunned down by terrorists and surely killed; an event the audience witnessed early in the film. However, Doc Brown holds information that the audience does not. Having read the letter that Marty gave him when he was in 1955, he is aware of the danger posed by the terrorists and is wearing a bullet-proof vest. This places a knowledge gap between the character of Doc Brown and the audience because Doc Brown holds knowledge that the audience does not have. The audience knows that Doc Brown has been gunned down and surely killed. They do not know he has prepared for this eventuality. The delayed exposition means the knowledge gap remains open for 70 minutes before the audience receives the information which Doc Brown had from the beginning.[2]

As a more complex example, the audience knows from the first act of *Back to the Future* how Marty's future father, George McFly (Crispin Glover) met his future mother Lorraine (Lea Thompson) when they were both seventeen in 1955. George was hit by Lorraine's father's car and taken unconscious into the house of his future grandparents. Lorraine cared for him, felt sorry for him, and she fell in love with him, the audience is informed, by virtue of the "Florence Nightingale effect" (dialogue from *Back to the Future*, 1985).

However, Marty's visit from 1985 to 1955 interferes with this fateful meeting. Marty saves his father from the predestined accident, but the car hits Marty instead of his father. Marty has replaced his future father both in that version of history and in his future mother's affections. Because George now does not meet Lorraine, and the Florence Nightingale effect cannot act on Lorraine's feelings towards George, the principal subplot is now initiated, requiring that Marty contrives a new way of getting his future parents to meet and fall in love. If Marty fails, he will not exist in the future. His first attempts to simply introduce them fail, so Marty is obliged to try something different. As Lorraine states that she wants "a strong man. A man who can protect the woman he loves" (dialogue from *Back to the Future*, 1985) the plan he comes up with is not based on Lorraine taking pity on an injured, weak and unassertive George, but by engaging in a pretend-fight with George, which George wins, they will trick Lorraine into thinking George is brave and strong. The plan works far better than Marty could have possible imagined, as George unexpectedly overcomes the bully, Biff Tannen (Thomas F. Wilson), and impresses Lorraine with his genuine courage.

---

[2] There are arguments in the logic of space-time continuity that contend Doc Brown did not have this information or the bullet-proof vest in act 1, but from the perspective of audience causal logic (and therefore knowledge gap dynamics) he did.

Marty's interference with the way his parents met has a profound effect on his father's assertiveness, his life and career, and, thereby, the consequent quality of the 1985 family thirty years later. As the audience discovers towards the latter stages of the film, when Marty eventually returns to 1985, all aspects of his family life are now of a higher quality, having been driven by a strong, assertive father for thirty years instead of a weak one. The gap between these two versions of events creates a revelation for the audience at the story resolution as they reel back through what they have experienced and make the connection between the different way that George met Lorraine and the impact that has on their lives in the new, improved version of 1985. The spectator figures this out and projects knowledge into the revelation gap they did not realise was there until they get back to 1985 and, along with Marty, see for themselves the profound changes in George and how those changes manifest in the family's 1985 quality of life.

4.3.1.2 Privilege gaps

Privilege gaps exist when the audience knows more than another participant. To continue with another aspect of the previous example, in *Back to the Future*, Marty makes a plan to help George to appear strong and impressive to Lorraine in order that she might fall in love with him (Lorraine having expressed her desire for a 'strong' man). The plan requires George to leave the Enchantment Under the Sea Dance at precisely 9.00pm and approach the parked car in which Marty is pretending to make inappropriate sexual advances towards Lorraine (very inappropriate — this is his future mother!). George is to play his part in the charade. He will drag Marty from the car and pretend to beat him up and apparently rescue Lorraine from Marty's molestations. However, the audience knows that things are not going to plan. As George approaches the car, it is the feared bully, Biff, (played by Thomas F. Wilson) making genuinely inappropriate advances towards Lorraine in the car, who will greet his arrival, not Marty as he expects. There is a gap whereby the audience is privileged with knowledge that Lorraine and George do not have. Lorraine knows nothing of the plan and George does not know that the plan has gone awry or that Biff is in the car.

There is another example of a different type of deep and pervasive privilege gap which characterises almost the entirety of *Back to the Future* from the moment Marty is accidentally sent back in time. After Marty arrives in 1955, he is effectively a time traveller from the future moving amongst the people of 1955. The audience knows this, but none of the characters from 1955 does. This secret is a knowledge gap. This may seem counter-intuitive, because the audience knows as much as Marty. However, there are still plenty of participants — the 1955 characters — who do not know, so this is privilege knowledge.

Although some knowledge gaps may be directly relatable primarily between two participants, such as one character lying to another, the receiver's perspective will always be asserted. They either know this is a lie (privilege dynamic), so have more knowledge than the deceived, or they are unaware it is a lie, so will receive the impact of the knowledge gap in revelation when it comes to light for them. Either way, the gap is there, and so carries power within the story.

As one further — perhaps somewhat glib — example, at the very beginning of a narration the author knows everything and the audience knows nothing. A narration is a matter of the author slowly, gradually feeding out information/knowledge over time; the pieces of a puzzle which the receiver pieces together. A narration is, in this sense, one complex revelation gap, divided into many dozens of smaller gaps over time.

All knowledge gaps are classified according to the audience position as either privilege gaps when the audience knows more than another participant or revelation gaps when the audience knows less than another participant.

4.3.2 Simple, Compound and Complex Knowledge Gaps

All knowledge gaps are classified as either simple, compound or complex.

> **Simple**
>
> A knowledge gap which is opened and closed within its own context and is not comprised of any other significant knowledge gaps is classed as a **simple** knowledge gap. For example, when Marty McFly knocks on the door to Doc's laboratory, the question is raised: 'Will Doc answer the door?' When Doc does answer the door, the question

is answered (the knowledge gap is closed) without other knowledge gaps requiring closure to resolve this one. It is therefore a simple knowledge gap. There are many hundreds of these through the course of a feature film.

Compound

A compound knowledge gap is one which comprises a number of simple knowledge gaps which must all achieve closure in order for the compound knowledge gap to be resolved.

When Marty arrives in 1955, he goes to a phone box and looks up Doc Brown's address. The compound knowledge gap is opened in the form of the question: 'Will Marty find Doc Brown in 1955?' In addressing this knowledge gap, Marty must first resolve a series of **simple** knowledge gaps, such as: Can he find out where Doc lives? Can he talk his future grandmother into letting him leave their house? Once that is achieved, can he find Riverside Drive? When he knocks on the door of a large house on Riverside: Will Doc Brown answer the door?

Complex

A complex knowledge gap is one that comprises at least two compound knowledge gaps, which must resolve for the complex knowledge gap to be resolved. For example, when Marty is accidentally sent back in time, the question is raised in the mind of the audience: 'Will Marty get back to 1985? How will he do it?' In addressing these questions, several compound knowledge gaps must be resolved, such as:

'Can Marty find Doc Brown?'

'Will Doc find a way to power the time machine?'

'Can Marty reunite his parents in love before he leaves 1955?'

In essence, simple knowledge gaps tend to equate with beats or short scenes, compound gaps with longer scenes or short sequences, and complex gaps with longer sequences, entire plots or subplots. The vast majority of stories are comprised of a mix of simple, compound and complex knowledge gaps.

4.4 Categories

With reference to the table above, the following five categories are addressed in detail through the body of this section:

1. **Paratext**: Knowledge gaps that foreshadow and surround the narrative but are not within the diegesis.
2. **Orientating diegetic gaps**: A receiver of a narration encounters 'orientating' knowledge gaps within the diegesis of the film. Gaps that are a part of the textual content, but which are more denoted, serving primarily to guide and direct the audience towards what the story is about.
3. **Mimetic orientating gaps:** Audience orientation still occurs within the mimesis (that is, audience orientation delivered by characters and their behaviours).
4. **Mimetic gaps:** Knowledge gaps which are contained in the actions and behaviours of the characters moving and living in their story world.
5. **Storification:** Knowledge gaps that result from a spectator's thoughts about narrated events, particularly with regard to the decisions made by characters and the consequences they reap as a result. The spectator's personal history and cultural understanding are required to interpret events and generate the subtext for themselves.

The receiver of a story first becomes aware of a film's existence through its paratext. They then become oriented to the viewing itself in the diegesis (the organised telling and receiver immersion), which includes the mimesis (the real-time action and words of the characters in their story world). As the story develops, the receiver will think about what they are experiencing and their feelings towards the story might change over time as other influences play their part; story meaning emerges in mind for the receiver as they bring their own thinking to bear on the production in mind; that is, storification takes place.

However, the story is never set in stone. Some paratext occurs after the film has finished, for example, through merchandise, extra features, discussing the film, re-watching the film, ongoing events in the lives of the stars, personal growth on the part of the receiver. Some orientation takes place at the overlap of the paratext and the diegesis (for example, the title and introductory music, and the font of the introductory credits), and storifications may be experienced during the narration as well as afterwards.

Note that there are not firm, scientific distinctions between these categories. They flow into one another with blurred boundaries. Many of the knowledge gaps identified can move between categories, reside in multiple categories or switch between them as things change over time. Stories and storytelling are aspects of art, not science, necessitating broad categorisations with type-placement chosen primarily through weighting and probability rather than absolutes.

4.4.1 Knowledge Gaps through Paratext

As touched upon earlier, paratext is information delivered through the material that pre-empts and surrounds the text, as introduced initially by Genette (1997), and later expanded on by Jonathan Gray (2010).

> A film (or any media text) is not defined solely by its diegetic content. The presence of any filmic or televisual text and its cultural impact, value and meaning cannot be adequately analysed without taking into account the film or program's many proliferations. Each proliferation, after all, holds the potential to change the meaning of the text, if only slightly. (Gray, 2010, p.2)

Paratext includes advertisements, billboards, discussion, previews and reviews, blogs, prequels, the book-of-the-film, trailers, interviews with involved personnel, entertainment news, magazine articles, merchandise, synergies, expert analysis, internet discussions and forums, official and unofficial web pages, promotions, posters, video games, DVD extras, bonus material and spin-offs. The text itself is only one part of the delivery of a narration. Gray (2010) argues that it is important to embrace 'off screen studies', as well as 'screen studies' to make sense of the wealth of other entities that saturate the media and form part of the narration. "Paratexts condition our entrance to texts, telling us what to expect, and setting the terms of our 'faith' in subsequent transubstantiation" (Gray, 2010, p.25).

There is still further paratext material at the entrance to the text itself: the title sequence, the font of the credits, the music over the credits, the promise in the star names, the lighting and mood. The material orientating the audience continues smoothly via these elements from the first paratextual encounter, which may be months or years earlier, gradually towards and into the diegesis itself.

4.4.2   Paratext and Knowledge Gaps

As a component of the narration, paratext opens (and fills) knowledge gaps. As the first knowledge that is made available towards a text is the paratext that foreshadows it, it follows that the first knowledge is characterised by questions that arise with that first awareness: 'What type of story is it? Who wrote it? Who stars in it? Is it about a character I know? Is it a story I feel I would like to experience?'

Paratext arrives with a receiver by accident or by design. Marketing and promotion may involve huge budgets and deeply considered psychology in order to attempt to resonate with a potential audience member. On the other hand, a star's behaviour in the real world can have a significant incidental knock-on effect on the way the public thinks about the films in which they feature. Either way, the paratext opens these sorts of knowledge gaps. Hence, the first knowledge gaps form (that is, the narration begins) for a potential receiver long before they open the book or enter a theatre. Quantifying the impact of paratext is challenging because there is an almost infinite range of paratexts, which may be deliberate or accidental, and may continue to be produced long after the text has been delivered. Each receiver experiences different types and quantities of paratext in their lives and processes it in unspecifiable ways. Additionally, the impression given by the whole story, including all paratext since the first publication or release and many proliferations, perhaps across many decades, changes over time. As Barbara

Klinger points out, there is no single impression, no single star image and no single ideology that can be fixed, and the mind-set of the audience cannot be known. All these things change diachronically. "[A]lmost all film historians are stuck in synchrony, focusing on the conjuncture in which films initially appeared to reveal their original circumstances of production, exhibition and reception" (Klinger, 1997, p.111-112).

Klinger exemplifies her point using Charles Maland's (1989) writing on the diachronic dimension to Charlie Chaplin and his work. During his years as an active star, particularly in America in the 1930s, Chaplin's perceived politics and dubious personal relationships negatively affected his image. However, Maland shows how the changing political climate of the 1960s and 1970s helped restore his reputation. Chaplin and his films were appreciated by a new generation in a more positive light, emphasising his creative talent over other factors. Nothing changed in Chaplin's oeuvre, but a new generation viewed his history differently, resulting in a new canonisation of his work (Maland, 1989, pp.317-360).

Chaplin also exemplifies how paratext can work. Imagine it is the 1930's and you hear that a new Charlie Chaplin film is coming out. What do you already know about that film? Your expectation is instantly set to the probability of a silent comedy, featuring his famous tramp character getting into scrapes with the police and figures of authority. And you would be right. With this knowledge, you are orientated towards the genre and mood with remarkable accuracy. The narration is already underway for you and your mindset orientated appropriately for the text, long before you even see the poster, let alone take a seat in the cinema.

Think about how much you know about the next Star Wars film, or James Bond adventure; or the next book you pick up by Lee Child or JK Rowling. Or how much you know about pretty much any film once you've seen the trailer. It is rare that we open page 1 or arrive in our cinema seats without being very well orientated to the upcoming story.

4.4.3 Knowledge Gaps in Diegetic Orientation

The paratext continues in the background as the main source of stimulation for the receiver moves to the diegesis — the delivery of the text itself. As you watch a film, anything that stimulates your senses that does not come from the audio-visual content is ongoing paratext. Indeed, given what was said earlier concerning the blurred boundary between categories, some of the diegesis may be considered to be paratext; the title sequence, for example. However, if that title sequence is delivered alongside or through characters in their story world the paratext and text overlap and the distinction between them becomes more nuanced. Take, for example, the use of intertitle boards in *Modern Times*. **Figure 13: Intertitle boards - text or paratext?** is an example intertitle board that occurs during the introductory sequence. Is this text or paratext?

Figure 13: Intertitle boards - text or paratext?

The answer is both. The title is part of the paratext. However, the contextual words can be considered part of the text, because they are delivering knowledge from within the story world. They are diegetic, and yet are orientating, and this is the category we will address now.

Within the diegesis, a number of knowledge gaps are opened up which still serve to orientate the receiver. Categorised as 'orientating diegetic knowledge gaps', these are knowledge gaps through: **Promise; Self-Conscious Narrator; Sound and Light; the Story World** and **Ellipsis Gaps.**

4.4.3.1 Knowledge Gaps through Promise

From the moment a receiver is engaged in the diegesis, they begin to gather and build the causal logic that constructs the story in mind. Whilst paratext has oriented the audience to an extent in advance of experiencing the text, there is also a great deal of material within the text that sets expectation and orientates the audience. Given a small stimulus, a receiver of a narration can be relied upon to project ahead; what Bell called the mind's "ineluctable compulsion to gestalt" (Bell, 1986, p.89). This tendency to overlay meaning onto anything and everything in the mise-en-scène opens up knowledge gaps through promise.

This is partly due to the "compulsion to gestalt" (ibid.) but is also due to the "subjective pact" (Macherey, 1966, p.71) between a writer and his audience. A receiver of story is looking to receive knowledge that the author is going to deliver. But the work is knowingly fighting against delivering reliable meaning. It is a declared fiction. And every story is presented in a manner that relentlessly hides its jewels; deliberate delay, distraction, red herrings, misdirection and all the other tools of the author's trade are utilised as part of the entertainment. No mystery story simply delivers its truth ('The Butler did it'). What would the point be in that?! No — there is a 'subjective pact' between the author and the audience that what is included in the narration, whilst deliberately leading the receiver a merry dance, will, ultimately, be worth the receiver's time, even if the value is not readily apparent moment by moment. For the author, this means that the audience is instantly engaged by the promise of just about every object, character, expression or event that features. Their 'compulsion to gestalt' makes everything immediately intriguing. As we shall see in several of the other knowledge gap types, many of them rely upon the tendency of the receiver to make assumptions and to speculate.

The mise-en-scène

In the context of film or theatre, the term *mise-en-scène* refers to everything that appears on the stage or before the camera, and its arrangement: composition, sets, props, actors, costumes, sound and light. Mise-en-scène also includes the positioning and movement of actors on the set. All these elements are available for audience interpretation, and all content is likely to be relevant at some point somewhere in the causal logic of the narrative. In this respect, all events, items and characters carry promise, and introduce knowledge gaps through that promise as the audience banks nuggets of potential and speculates on the future significance of each element. The spectator's construction of a story will project roles for any person, event or object and hold them in the mind ready to link them into the causal logic as soon as even vaguely reasonable connections can be made.

In the opening sequence of *Back to the Future,* an unexplained focus is placed on a case of plutonium hidden under a chair in Doc Brown's house. Even though the role of plutonium in Marty's teenage world is barely imaginable, there is promise in the plutonium's presence and, particularly, through the focalisation it is afforded. It later transpires that it takes plutonium to power the time machine, and that it was Doc Brown who stole the plutonium (leading to the tragic encounter with the terrorists and the accidental time travel that sends Marty back to 1955 in the first place). Further, the difficulty in procuring fresh supplies of plutonium in 1955 is what traps Marty there and renders him unable to return easily to 1985. The promise of the plutonium in this early sequence is realised in the causal logic of the narrative, and so becomes a component of the fabula from the moment it is first shown. However, because its role is not initially related to existing knowledge or events, it is part of the orientation of the audience to future elements, rather than having an immediately understood role in the story from the first exposure. It is a 'detached' component of the fabula, held there in mind, floating and awaiting other knowledge to connect up into meaning that involves the plutonium.

Whenever an audience is exposed to new events, characters or objects, a knowledge gap is opened up by the promise it holds. It is a gap that is filled once its role in the narrative's causal logic becomes clear.

4.4.3.2   Knowledge gaps through Self-Conscious Narrator

Of the narrative modes discussed in **section 2.2.7 - Modes of Narration**, the **self-conscious narrator** is a narrational mode delivering diegetic orientation to the viewer. The narrator fills and opens knowledge gaps, but it is not part of the mimesis of the story delivery. The narrator may be unidentified (as in *Jules et Jim* [1962]), or, more commonly, is one of the characters narrating from an 'all knowing, invisible' position (Sternberg, 1978, pp.56-57) explicitly delivering knowledge to the audience. An example is in *Sunset Boulevard* (1950; directed by Billy Wilder) in which Joe Gillis (William Holden) narrates his own story from beyond the grave. Other forms of delivery fulfil the same function, such as the use of intertitle boards in *Modern Times* which orientate the viewer to the change of time, space or situation, or the use of a news reporter to provide backstory in *Citizen Kane* (1941).

4.4.3.3 Knowledge Gaps through Sound and Light

Light and sound (excluding dialogue, which is addressed separately) are information streams that form part of the overall sensory experience of a film narration, and, as with any information source, can be manipulated to open and fill knowledge gaps between the expectation set by the music, sounds or lights and the actuality that unfolds. For example, portentous music and dark lighting could have an audience overlaying suspicion on a character who turns out later to be innocent. Although the range of narrative anticipation or recollection is more limited than with other types of gap in causal logic, these elements are still able to open and fill knowledge gaps.

> The classical film score enters into a system of narration, endowed with some degree of self-consciousness, a range of knowledge and a degree of communicativeness [...] The score can be omniscient, what Parker Tyler has called "a vocal apparatus of destiny". (Bordwell, 1985a, p.34)

Imagine a character with a facial expression that is serious. Now overlay upbeat music. They may now appear as though they are about to realise how wonderful this turn of events has transpired to be. Now overlay dark strings with a minor chord. That same facial expression now portents imminent disaster. Now overlay oompah music and the same facial expression could be seen as the incongruous po-face of a stand-up comic. Music, sound and lights are tools that can deliver information, and can therefore be part of knowledge, and knowledge gap, delivery.

One common knowledge gap of this form comes through the association of a sound or motif with a given character, action or moment. Once that association has been established, the mood can be recalled or the characteristic overlaid by a recapitulation of the motif. The story of *Peter and the Wolf* (1936, composed by Sergei Prokofiev) can be recounted entirely through music once the themes have been established. A more manifest example is the theme from *Jaws* (1975, directed by Spielberg; score by John Williams), which gives the audience the understanding that the shark is nearby even when there are no other clues to the shark's presence. In *The Big Sleep* (1946), the private detective, Marlowe (Humphrey Bogart), is staking out a house when there is suddenly a scream, a gunshot and a flash of light from within. These sounds and lights raise urgent questions (open important knowledge gaps) for Marlowe and for the audience. Even though we do not see a woman or a gun, we fill the gaps from the given sounds and lights.

In *Back to the Future*, sound and light are used to provide the audience with an understanding that time travel is taking place. As the DeLorean time machine hits 88 miles-per-hour, it becomes adorned with neon blue lights accompanied by a specific orchestral theme in the score by John Williams. Both these aspects of sound and light only occur when the time machine journeys through time. A blinding white flash and the disappearance of the time machine from the mise-en-scène complete the routine, which the audience comes to understand indicates that time travel has taken place.

The lighting and music are rarely given the credit they deserve for the contribution they make to the sum of knowledge. After all, your ears represent fifty percent of the sensory apparatus used for most cinematic narrations. As George Antheil (cited in Morton, 1950, p.4-5) commented, "the characters in a film drama never know what is going to happen to them, but the music always knows".

4.4.3.4 The Story World

As established in section 1, many of the assumptions we make about the real world come from generally accurate expectations regarding what the world is likely to offer us. The world in which we live and move has been experienced many times before, so the mind loads it up as a 'given' that can be taken for granted in the sense that the unconscious mind sets the expectation and the monitoring of core consciousness simply confirms that all is fulfilling expectation.

This is why simply visiting a new town, as a tourist for example, is stimulating. Our most fundamental expectations are rebuilt around the characters, objects and events that characterise this new environment. Visiting an environment with its own narrative and characters — say a zoo, sports stadium or hospital — involves a great deal more of our higher cognitive functions if we are going to understand the narratives of this new 'world' and thrive.

The same is true of story. It is highly stimulating to be taken to experience a new 'world', and important to the fundamental understanding of what is going on that the new world is clear to the receiver of the story. When we are taken to 1955 in *Back to the Future*, or to a new planet in *Star Trek*, to life 30-million years into the future in *The Time Machine* (1895, written by HG.Wells), to the world of drug-dealers in *Breaking Bad*, the fictional underwater world of *SpongeBob Squarepants,* the Hogwart's School of Witchcraft and Wizardry in *Harry Potter* — it is a new experience to visit that world and to fill the knowledge gaps that lead to understanding its natural laws.

As the world and its laws are delivered, this represents knowledge, and therefore fills knowledge gaps. The story world is highly important in orientating the audience and can be a delightful and powerful source of new knowledge and impactful stimulation for the receiver.

4.4.3.5 Ellipsis Gaps

According to Bordwell, a narrative comprises representations of three systems: the representation of time, space and causal logic (Bordwell, 1985a, pp.12-60). Ellipsis gaps quantify the manipulation of time, and often a change of space.

The 'narrative ellipsis' was first described by Genette, (1980, pp.86-113). An ellipsis gap is created when the story skips over the events in a protagonist's life which the perceiver can construct for themselves in the fabula without having them delivered in the narration.

For example, if we see an evidently pregnant woman in one scene, and in the next scene she is caring for a baby, our "ineluctable compulsion to gestalt" (Bell, 1986, p.89) will have us do the writerly work in the gap in time that has been placed here. We link these events into a narrative for these characters across the months which have been skipped. This will include the drama and emotion of a childbirth which, whilst evidently part of the syuzhet and the fabula, was not featured in the narration. In this way, a film with a two-hour duration can encompass a fabula that runs across a hundred years. *Back to the Future* encompasses the lives of the main characters across a period of thirty years, taking George and Lorraine from the age of 17 to the age of 47. However, all the necessary story information is delivered in a narration of less than two hours. When narrative manipulates the chronological order or duration of story events through editing techniques, such as cross-cutting and flashback, the audience generally has no problem in making accurate assumptions concerning what happened in the omitted time period and building the intended story in mind.

Gerald Prince (1988, pp.1-5) divided the ellipsis gap into what he called the **non-narrated,** the **dis-narrated** and the **un-narratable**. From my perspective, these represent three types of gaps in knowledge that comprise information which is "unmentioned or unmentionable" for the receiver of a narration.

- **Non-narrated:** Any component of the syuzhet which is missed out. Periods of time or events of detail which occurred, but the omission of which does not disrupt the causal logic of the story. For example, if a man walks along the street, the minutiae of his foot movement relative to his knee on each and every step is not documented. It is essential in its own way, of course, but can be assumed to take place and is not required information in the creation of an appropriate fabula element, so is non-narrated.
- **Dis-narrated:** All those many possibilities which could have happened (but did not) or which did not happen (but could have). A story can only take one of the myriad possible paths. Consideration of all the possible alternatives is not necessary or useful, so is missed; however, it is often relevant to consider the choices made in the light of those that were options.

- **Un-narratable:** Any element of a story that is omitted due to, for example, taboo, legal, cultural or ideological restrictions, such as the impact of the Hays Code (a moral code asserted over filmmakers in the USA between 1930 and 1968) or other ideologically pragmatic reasons ruling it out, such as the way that genre convention excludes material.

These may not appear to be very relevant. However, the intrigue in a story or event often comes from a character having to make a *choice*. As an audience we are all too aware of the risk a character is taking when they choose one path to follow rather than another, and when the chosen path is not the one we would recommend or wish to take for ourselves (or vicariously on behalf of our hero), then we are experiencing engagement in the story. In a sense, what is not done and the choices not made provide the context and contrast for what is chosen, and therein lies the engagement. Do not forget that we are looking for holes, not for netting, in which case, ellipsis gaps are the largest and most numerous gaps of all, providing a context for everything that is not the narration. As Bell points out, "a story is a tiny representative part of the inexhaustible whole which can never be fully told." (Bell, 1986, pp.85). The potential in the entire syuzhet, even for a single story, is immeasurable. The potential in the fabula is similarly and equivalently beyond measure — we simply do not know how much of the (unspecifiable) syuzhet is interpreted into equivalent fabula phenomena mind by any given receiver.

In using a knowledge gap approach in data gathering and classification for a specific narration, the main ellipsis gaps can be documented (that is, for example, the edits between scenes causing jumps in time or sudden changes in location) as they have a role to play in delineating what is relevant to the story (and they implicitly define the non-narrated); however, no attempt will be made to apprehend the immeasurable detail of the dis-narrated and the un-narratable.

4.4.4 Orientating Gaps in Mimetic Text Events

Within the diegesis comes the mimesis, and this mode of narration has knowledge gaps that can be categorised in two forms. This first category captures knowledge gaps that are functions of the mimesis; that is, delivered by the actions, words and behaviours of the characters as they live and move in their story world. However, at this point we are still restricting the knowledge gap types within this category to those which are functioning to orientate the audience to the direction and purpose of the story.

These are knowledge gaps through: **Questions (Key Questions, Event Questions); Character Plans; Motivation; Conflict; Harmatia; Backstory;** and **Education**.

4.4.4.1 Knowledge gaps through Questions

Any question is implicitly a gap in knowledge, so a principal method of opening a knowledge gap and keeping it open is to have the events of the story raise questions in the mind of the audience. As Bordwell suggests:

> In the course of constructing the story, the perceiver uses schemata [scripts] and incoming cues to make assumptions, draw inferences about current story events, and frame and test hypotheses about prior and upcoming events. (Bordwell, 1985b, p.35) Our hypothesis-forming activity can be thought of as a series of questions which the text impels us to ask (Bordwell, 1985a, p.39).

A narrative dynamic based on raising a question has been a recurrent factor in influential theories. Barthes (1990) frames the raising and answering of questions as the Hermeneutic Code. He also explains how questions may be direct (for example, characters asking each other questions that the story events must address) or they can be indirect when inferred from the dialogue and action. Importantly, Barthes also identified the importance for a narration when a question is raised and left unanswered for deliberately long periods.

> The problem is to maintain the enigma in the initial void of its answer; whereas the sentences quicken the story's 'unfolding' and cannot help but move the story along, the hermeneutic code performs an opposite action: it must set up delays (obstacles, stoppages, deviations) in the flow of the discourse; its structure is essentially reactive, since it opposes the ineluctable advance of language with an organized set of stoppages: between question and answer there is a whole dilatory area whose emblem might be named 'reticence'. (Barthes, 1990, p.75)

To put the same dynamic in my terms, a question is a knowledge gap, and deliberately leaving it open (unanswered) for extended periods is a technique for ensuring audience engagement.

Because questions manifest at each of the simple, compound and complex classifications they have been divided into three knowledge gap types: Key Questions (complex in form); Event Questions (compound in form); and Hermeneutic Questions (simple in form).

Key Questions (Complex Form)

A key question comprises a series of complex and compound knowledge gaps. In constructing a knowledge gap through a key question, the gap is held open across an extended period in which a series of compound knowledge gaps (and even further complex knowledge gaps) are opened. These must be addressed and closed out before the key question can be resolved. In this way, key questions are often used to provide a story's major dramatic arcs. For example, in contemporary Hollywood terminology, the key question is raised by an inciting incident, and that key question is answered at the story's climax. As McKee argues:

> In Hollywood jargon, the central plot's Inciting Incident is the "big hook" [...] the event that incites and captures the audience's curiosity. Hunger for the answer to the Major Dramatic Question grips the audience's interest, holding it until the last act's climax. (McKee, 1998, p.198)

The key question, by virtue of its complex composition, is one that remains unanswered across the wider arcs of the story and, therefore, orientates the audience to the story's main plot, major subplot or longer sequences. In *Back to the Future* Marty McFly is accidentally sent back in time to 1955. The narrative makes it clear that he did not intend for this to happen, and the audience is given to understand that he does not want to stay there; his life has been thrown out of balance. This is an inciting incident which raises a key question: 'Will Marty get home to 1985?' And, given that the time machine is broken and the necessary fuel (plutonium) cannot be found in 1955: 'How will he do it?'

Knowing the wider aims of the story and the goals and motivation of the protagonist also helps an audience, in orientation terms, to accurately project fabula constructs because these goals and motivation provide a framework for causal logic. If you see a man running as fast as he possibly can, your instinct is to frame that within a context. You wish to know *why* he is running so frantically. This is a gap in your knowledge and you feel compelled to fill that gap. If you then notice that the chap is wearing shorts and running with others along a track towards a finish line, now we have our context, the frantic running makes sense, and our mind becomes satisfied. The question now morphs into 'who is going to win?' Knowledge gaps often only make sense relative to some baseline, and the key question is a common method to provide a solid context across a story's wide arcs.

This is one reason for the popularity of crime stories. As soon as you know a detective is on the case, you have your context for everything that happens; that relative baseline against which all actions and choices are contextualised. You know what the story is about and why characters are there. Everything that happens is considered in the context of the protagonist's wider aim: to uncover and apprehend the criminal. Every moment in the story is therefore considered in this light whenever the audience gets new information and projects forwards.

Knowledge Gaps through Event Questions (Compound Form)

The same dynamic is at play in an event question as it is for the key question, the difference being that an event question is a **compound** knowledge gap. The knowledge gap that is opened comprises a number of **simple** knowledge gaps that must resolve before the event question can be resolved.

The knowledge gap that is opened is, therefore, mostly associated with orientating the audience to the aims of a scene or sequence. The question is raised but becomes dependent upon other simple knowledge gaps being resolved before it can be resolved. In *Modern Times*, each time the Tramp gets a new job, the event question is raised: 'Will he be able to keep this job?' (*Modern Times*, 1936). This provides the repeated model for the story's seven set piece comedy sequences. A number of simple knowledge gaps are opened and resolved across a number of scenes before the event question is answered. He inevitably loses his job and the knowledge gap is closed.

Hermeneutic Questions (Simple Form)

Hermeneutic questions complete the set of knowledge gap types through questions. However, as hermeneutic questions are generally mimetic, they are addressed in detail in section 4.4.5 — Knowledge Gaps in Text Events.

4.4.4.2 Knowledge Gaps through Character Plans

A specific version of the mimetic orientation dynamic occurs when characters make plans. Again, Barthes (1990, p.18) provides us with a basis for something akin to this knowledge gap with the Proairetic Code, which applies to any action that implies a further narrative action. If a character pulls a pin from a hand grenade, a certain expectation is set for what may happen next. A plan is a more sophisticated version of this dynamic; indeed, it simultaneously seeds three knowledge gaps.

A plan delivers the audience a 'given' hypothesis against which the action can be compared as events unfold. In *Back to the Future*, Marty's future father, George, is weak and unassertive. This is a problem for Marty, as his future mother, Lorraine, has expressed her desire for a strong, assertive man. You will remember from our earlier use of this example that Marty and George make a plan, based around a role play that will convince Lorraine that George is the type of strong man she desires. Lorraine is infatuated with Marty at the time, so their plan involves Marty taking Lorraine to the school dance. At precisely 9.00pm, Marty will be making inappropriate sexual advances towards Lorraine in the car. George will turn up just in time, rip the car door open and say, "Hey you. Get your damn hands off her." (dialogue from *Back to the Future,* 1985) George will drag Marty from the car, punch him in the stomach, and rescue Lorraine, who will be so impressed with George's apparent strength and assertiveness that she will fall in love and the fated path necessary for Marty to be born in 1968 will be back on track. Indeed, we are told that George and Lorraine must kiss on the dancefloor for history to be back on track, so this setting of the plan works like a key question: Will George and Lorraine kiss on the dancefloor?

The audience understands the plan and its aims and is, therefore, orientated to the intended path the story will take if things go to plan (a privilege dynamic). However, as the story continues into the sequences in which the plan is implemented, George's nemesis, the bully, Biff, contrives to be in the car in place of Marty. As George approaches the car, the audience is aware that the plan is not going as intended. There is a gap between the path the plan was intended to take and actual events; there is a gap between the characters' situation as the plan plays out and the aims the plan is intended to achieve; and there is a gap between those participants who know of the plan and those who do not.

Hence, knowledge gaps through character plans manifest in three ways:

   a) As a basis for audience hypothesis. The character making the plan has a goal or aim implicit to that plan. The viewer accepts the achievement of this goal as one of the questions driving the story (will the plan work?) and so is orientated to the characters' broader objectives.
   b) As a baseline for knowledge gaps in text events that occur when actual events deviate from the intended plan. There are knowledge gaps opened between what happens in the mimesis and what the audience knows was supposed to happen in the plan.
   c) In the knowledge gap between those that know of the plan and those that do not. The audience will always be situated in one of these two positions, thereby rendering the plan either a privilege or a revelation gap. Although it is most common for the audience to know of the plan, it is equally engaging to deploy a plan with a revelation dynamic. The audience becomes intrigued by the actions of the protagonist, wondering what they are up to until the knowledge builds to a point that the plan becomes evident.

4.4.4.3 Knowledge Gaps through Motivation

As soon as a character's motivation is known, it is linked to aims and outcomes that will define the satisfaction of that motivation. The receiver will predict the actions and behaviours that are likely to be required to achieve those aims and outcomes and the question is raised in the mind of the receiver: Will the character achieve fulfilment in these terms? How will they go about it?

Marty McFly did not want to go to 1955 and the audience becomes aware that, for him, fulfilment means getting back to his life in 1985. His motivation acts as a baseline against which plans can be made and judged; actions and events can be measured and contextualised; obstacles, conflicts and forces of antagonism can be set.

As soon as a character's motivation is known, a knowledge gap is opened up between their current situation and a desired outcome in which fulfilment has been achieved in the context of that motivation.

4.4.4.4 Knowledge Gaps through Conflict

As a character's motivation drives them towards fulfilment, there are likely to be forces of antagonism providing barriers to achieving their aims and goals. This causes conflict in the story. As soon as there is conflict there is a knowledge gap in the questions regarding how the protagonist will overcome the forces of antagonism that are causing the conflict. Will the protagonist win or lose as a result of the conflict?

When one thinks of conflict one thinks of 'bad guys' and of course relationship conflicts are the most common form. However, forces of antagonism can come in many forms, such as an internal conflict (doubts and insecurities within an individual, such as George McFly's battle with his own cowardice); institutional conflict (difficulties in the rules of, for example, the law of the land, school rules, doctors and hospitals, bookmakers, banks and so on). There are practical conflicts with, for example, the rules of society, the laws of physics, technology or electricity, the unavoidable impact of illness or pregnancy, and the sci-fi rules of your story world, such as those concerned with time travel. Then there are additional possibilities for antagonism from factors completely outside of the control of the protagonist, such as weather events, acts of fate, God or mother nature, random acts of third party characters, accidents and coincidences.

Whenever there is conflict there is a gap in the question: Which of the forces involved in the conflict will win out? How will that happen?

4.4.4.5 Knowledge Gaps through Harmatia

Aristotle outlined three key aspects of story in his *Poetics* (Aristotle, 335BC [1996]) known as the *harmatia, anagnorisis* and *peripeteia*. Each of these carries an implicit knowledge gap. These are addressed in detail in **section 4.4.5.11 - Knowledge gaps through Aristotle Principles**.

Suffice to say at this point that the harmatia is a 'mistake' or error' which throws the protagonist's world out of balance. Rather like an inciting incident, it raises a question in the mind of the receiver: How will the protagonist return their life to balance?

4.4.4.6 Knowledge Gaps through Education

Kendall Haven argues that the receivers of information:

> [Firstly...] more readily comprehend and retain key information and concepts when they are presented in story form. [...] Stories form the framework and structure though which humans sort, understand, relate and file experience into memory. Story structure is how we view the world; it is how we place information into memory; it is how we recall information into consciousness (Haven, 2007, p.90, 118).

As discussed in section 1, there is growing evidence to suggest that stories exist as they do and carry their power to grip and intrigue because they are a tangible representation of the modes of operation of the human mind.[3]

Haven continues:

> More than just being a uniquely effective learning, teaching and communications tool [...] the reason behind this unique effectiveness is that stories match how humans naturally perceive, process, think and learn (Haven, 2007, p.103).

Stories educate in multiple ways. When a story delivers direct, denoted information this implicitly fills in a knowledge gap for all those who did not have that information in the first place. This would be a predominant form of knowledge gap in, for example, the creation of a documentary; *The Story of*

---

[3] For more on this, see, for example, Branigan (1992); Bordwell (1985b); McRaney (2012); Cohen & Martin (2008).

Medicine or *The Story of Steam Power*. However, education can also be a component of a fictional story. In *Some Like it Hot*, a receiver could learn something about, for example, prohibition and the activities of the mob in the USA in 1929 (*Some Like it Hot*, 1959).

In this way, every story educates through providing insights into culture, attitudes and politics by taking us to another time and place, as discussed in the story world. *Modern Times* gives us a representation of life in 1930s America while *The Big Sleep* shows us 1946 and *Back to the Future* provides a depiction of 1955 and 1985. These are not entirely representative but they deliver knowledge all the same, on fashion, transport, politics, attitudes and so on. Do not forget that a story 'truth' does not have to be something factual in the real world. It is merely a component of a narrative that makes sense and therefore has meaning.

A narration also depicts the consequences of behaviours and decisions in the spectators' minds as they follow the causal logic of characters' actions and appreciate the outcomes. Moreover, stories can teach the receiver of a story lessons concerning appropriate behaviours for social situations, such as the moral message inherent in a children's story (addressed in **section 4.4.6 — Knowledge Gaps through Storification**).

There is education within the diegesis, but a film also educates us to the real world, cultural attitudes and film-making at the time and the circumstances in which the film was made. *Some Like it Hot,* whilst set in 1929, is a story concerned with alternative gender constructs and provides insights into the gender politics of 1959. Again, such 'education' may or may not be the truth, but it is still delivered and it still manifests as knowledge in the receiver's mind, just like any other. For example, forms of education orientate the audience to the laws of the story world. In *Back to the Future,* it is important to the story that the laws of time travel are understood. Without the imperative that 1.21 gigawatts of power are required to facilitate time travel at precisely 88 miles-per-hour, which can only be sourced in 1955 by a bolt of lightning, much of the intrigue and tension of the story would be removed. Audiences leave *Back to the Future* 'knowing' that it takes 1.21 gigawatts of electricity to power time-travel. This knowledge is 'reliable meaning' in the context of enjoying the film story even though it is not a fact in the real world.

4.4.4.7 Knowledge Gaps through Backstory

Backstory provides knowledge from the history of the story world that is brought to bear within a relevant, wider knowledge gap within the mimesis. Hence, for example, when Lorraine tells her family in 1985 the detailed story of how she met their father in 1955, this is historical information that is relevant to the later events when Marty's knowledge of this backstory (for example, that *the Enchantment Under the Sea Dance* is the scene of his parents' first kiss) has a significant impact on a real-time, mimetic knowledge gap.

4.4.5 Knowledge Gaps in Text Events

This section lists the knowledge gaps that are generated through the actions, words and behaviours of the characters moving before us as they live out real-time events in their story world. That is, the knowledge gaps that are delivered mimetically. These are knowledge gaps through: **Hermeneutic Questions, Subterfuge, Subplot, Actions and Dialogue, Suggestion and Implication, Suspense, Misinterpretation and Misdirection, Comedy, Distraction, Mise-en-scène, and Aristotle's Principles**.

4.4.5.1 Knowledge Gaps through Hermeneutic Questions

Hermeneutic questions are of the **simple** knowledge gap classification, meaning that they are opened and resolved within their own dramatic context. They have the same foundations in Barthes' (1990, p.75) Hermeneutic Code as the compound and complex question types identified in the orientating category, identifying any form of question or enigma.

> From a constructivist standpoint, people perform operations on a story. When information is missing, perceivers infer it or make guesses about it. [They] seek causal connections among events, both in anticipation and in retrospect (Bordwell, 1985b, p.34)

In performing such operations, the audience is constantly working in interpretive mode, raising questions in their own mind and answering them with reasoned hypotheses. Bordwell continues:

> Our hypothesis-forming activity can be thought of as a series of questions which the text impels us to ask (Bordwell, 1985a, p.39).

And, of course, all questions open a knowledge gap in the mind of the spectator. The simple type of question is also generally mimetic and of short duration. It therefore does not orientate the audience towards the wider arcs of the story and is, therefore, included in this section rather than in with the compound and complex question types.

In *Back to the Future*, when Marty McFly knocks on the door of Doc Brown's house on Riverside Drive, his action raises the event question in mind: Will Doc Brown answer the door? Doc Brown does indeed answer the door, and this **simple** knowledge gap is closed without having to resolve any other knowledge gaps.

4.4.5.2   Knowledge Gaps through Actions and Dialogue

Actions and words are the substance of mimesis, delivering the behaviours and interactions of the characters (or psychologically motivated 'causal agents' as Bordwell [1985b, p.157] calls them) as they live and move before the audience. A spectator will judge and evaluate every action and every word, searching them for meaning and subtext, just as they do the actions and words of people with whom they interact in their real lives. That search is a function of an implicit knowledge gap:

a) **Action**: A player takes an action, and the audience may speculate (rightly or wrongly) a potential story development. In *Back to the Future* when Marty McFly runs into the road in 1955 and saves his future father from being hit by a car, he, Marty, is knocked unconscious by the impact instead of his father. This action opens wide ranging knowledge gaps into which the audience may project. Marty has replaced his father in his father's life and is about to meet his own future mother instead of George meeting his future wife. Lorraine falls for Marty instead of George and now Marty will not exist in the future unless he can get the romance between Lorraine and George back on track. How will he do it? What will happen?

b) **Dialogue**: The words characters say have a surface meaning, which will be interpreted in the context of the story at that moment. However, there may also be a gap between the literal meaning of the words and the character's intent, between that literal meaning and another character's perception, or between that meaning and the audience's perception. No dialogue is truth and, indeed, no dialogue can immediately be trusted as reliable meaning.

In *Back to the Future* when Biff grabs George by the lapels and tells him: "If I hand my homework in in your handwriting, I'd get kicked outta school. You wouldn't want that to happen, would ya?" After a telling hesitation, George replies: "Oh, no, of course not, Biff. I wouldn't want that to happen" (Dialogue from *Back to the Future*, 1985). There is a gap here between the literal meaning of George's spoken words and the underlying meaning. George's words are saying that he would not want Biff to be thrown out of school, and yet the audience is left in little doubt that George would be very pleased indeed if Biff got thrown out of school.

In an example with a different dynamic, Marty's future mother, Lorraine, is watching him outwit the bullies. She turns to her friends and declares: "He's such a dreamboat!" (ibid.). From her actions and words, the audience perceives that she is romantically attracted to her own son. There is a knowledge gap between the audience understanding of Lorraine's aims in life through this knowledge and the perception of Marty and Doc Brown, who do not realise the problems that are developing through this attraction. Nor do they realise that the more Marty stands up to the bully to help his future father, the more Lorraine becomes infatuated with him instead of George. Thus, through these four spoken words, a gap is introduced between what the audience knows and what Marty and Doc know.

Knowledge gaps are introduced through a difference between the actions and words of the characters and the possible differing interpretations of those actions and words by the different participants in the story, depending upon the knowledge they have.

In analytical terms, counting knowledge gaps of this type is challenging for several reasons. As has been established, all action and dialogue require interpretation, from the minutiae of the signs and signifiers, through the cultural input that creates significations, right up into the event-level context of the causal logic of the story, its narrafications and storifications. The knowledge gaps that are opened and filled through action and dialogue are continuous and innumerable. Action and words come together to create larger phenomenological entities in mind, just as they do in the real world. In this respect, actions and words are often the *agency* delivering <u>information</u> that creates a gap of another kind, rather than the <u>knowledge</u> that harbours the gap. Dialogue might create a knowledge gap through backstory; action might create a moment of comedy; the words spoken may create a plan or subterfuge. For this reason, knowledge gaps through action and words are surprisingly low in number in a content analysis.

4.4.5.3 Knowledge gaps through Subterfuge

Knowledge gaps are implicit to any form of subterfuge. A character's true motivation or agenda is hidden from other characters who may later be impacted by that motivation or agenda. A gap exists between the audience knowledge of the subterfuge and the knowledge held by the owner or the victims of the subterfuge. Propp's functions of story include several (namely, functions 4, 6 and 23) involving a disguise or switched identity (Propp, 1928; pp. 15,39,32). In each case, the disguise, masquerade or subterfuge includes a gap in knowledge between the character in disguise and those that are fooled by it. In creating a knowledge gap, subterfuge does not necessarily require lies and deceit (although these are valid examples); it may also be implicit to the character or their process, such as a superhero's alter ego. Any knowledge withheld by a character from another participant, even if the audience is aware of the deception, is a knowledge gap through subterfuge.

Below are two examples from *Back to the Future*. Both depict knowledge gaps through subterfuge. One exemplifies a privilege classification and the other, revelation:

a) The fact that Marty McFly is a time traveller from the future throughout his time in 1955 is a knowledge gap through subterfuge. The audience knows the truth, as does Marty, but nobody else in 1955 does, and this creates a (privilege) knowledge gap through subterfuge.

b) When Doc Brown is shot multiple times in the chest by terrorists in the early parts of the film, he is wearing a bullet-proof vest. The audience, along with Marty, is unaware of this. At climax, we find out that he had heeded Marty's warnings in 1955, he was wearing a protective vest and so survives the shooting. This is a (revelation) knowledge gap through subterfuge.

4.4.5.4 Knowledge Gaps through Subplot

Barthes built on the concept of cause leading to effect in constructing his Proairetic Code. The code labels actions which encourage the viewer to use their predictive capability to "rationally [...] determine the result of an action" (Barthes, 1990, p.18). There is an implicit knowledge gap when an event implies that an outcome or result can be rationally predicted, and that in turn creates suspense as the viewer waits to find out if the predicted action or event manifests.

In the case of knowledge gaps through subplot, actions in one plotline potentially cause the audience to reconfigure their assumptions and projections about what logically may now happen in the progression of another plotline.

In *Back to the Future* when Marty interferes with the meeting between his parents in 1955, the audience realises that there is no point in his achieving his overarching story aim (to time-travel his way back home to 1985) because if his parents do not meet in 1955, he will not exist when he gets back to the future. Hence, there are now two plotlines:

a) The main plot storyline, with the key question: Can Marty successfully get home to 1985?

b) The subplot storyline, with the key question: Can Marty re-unite his parents in love before he returns to 1985?'

The two plotlines are interdependent. As Marty sets about contriving his parents' meeting, the audience is interpreting events in this subplot storyline in the context of their implications for the main plot storyline (of which his future parents, of course, have no inkling). Similarly, progress in the main plot storyline is interpreted in the context of its impact on the subplot storyline. For example, the knowledge that the bolt of lightning which will power his journey back to 1985 in the main plot line is at a fixed point in time on the Saturday night is brought to bear on events in the subplot in which Marty is attempting to reunite his parents in love. Every subplot event is overshadowed by the time limits imposed by the imperatives of the main plot. Additionally, the outcome of the main plot, as and when Marty makes it back to 1985, is inextricably linked to progress in the subplot. Indeed, ultimately, these two plots directly intertwine at climax. Marty's actions in the romantic fortunes of his parents in the subplot in 1955 have an unexpected and profoundly positive effect on his life as it is later revealed to be in the main plotline back in 1985.

The gap between the projections made due to events in one plotline on the outcomes in a second plotline is a knowledge gap through subplot.

4.4.5.5 Knowledge gaps through Implication and Suggestion

There are many tools of implication and suggestion. The clothes someone wears may suggest their profession, wealth, personality, recent or intended likely behaviour. The soundtrack or lighting can tip the audience towards a mood or characteristic. A facial expression or a movement of a curtain can have the audience infer information and project forwards on that basis. And this basis may transpire to be true or false. Just because a man is wearing a policeman's uniform does not mean he is a policeman. Even if he can prove he is a policeman, that does not mean he is necessarily honest.

A simple example would be the monster terrifying the occupants of the spacecraft in *Alien* (1979, directed by Ridley Scott). The monster does not make a physical appearance until three-quarters of the way through the film. The rest of the time, its presence and awesome powers are all implied rather than spelled out, leaving it up to the imagination of the receiver to project a monster, idealised in the mind as a result of being unseen. Audience imagination is relied upon to do a better job of building a monster that genuinely unsettles them than any purveyor of computer-generated mayhem and teeth. For most of the film we see nothing but ceiling tiles rattling and images on radar screens, and because the knowledge is so lacking, the audience generates subtext through implication and makes the monster larger than life for themselves.

It is a similar story with the shark in *Jaws* (1975, directed by Steven Spielberg). It is a highly rated movie, but, the shark that was responsible for so much fear and contributed immeasurably to the reputation of great whites around the world is not seen in full on screen until we are some 80 minutes into the film. Particularly these days, the shark is only scary before you see it. Given modern capabilities to generate CGI realism, seeing that plastic shark is pretty much a joke; however, even today, not seeing it remains powerful.

The gap between the audience's projected understanding and the actuality is a knowledge gap through implication or suggestion. As Bordwell explains:

> "so ongoing and insistent is the perceiver's drive to anticipate narrative information that a confirmed hypothesis easily becomes a tacit assumption, the ground for further hypothesis" (Bordwell, 1985b, p.38).

In *Back to the Future*, when Doc Brown asks to view the photograph of Marty standing with his siblings, his older brother, Dave (Marc McClure) is fading from the photograph. The implication is that the decreasing likelihood that George and Lorraine will ever become romantically involved and have children is gradually beginning to erase the family from existence, one by one in order of birth. This photograph is used regularly throughout the narration, filling a knowledge gap through implication that provides a context for the possibility of Marty existing in the future.[4]

4.4.5.6 Knowledge Gaps through Misinterpretation or Misdirection

In a similar manner to implication and suggestion, a writer can use the tendency of the audience to draw inferences from limited information in projecting future outcomes by twisting events and forcing the audience to rethink their projections and reconfigure their hypotheses. In some cases, the

---

[4] When Marty is saying goodbye to his future parents just before he finally leaves 1955, he has reunited them in love and his future mother says thoughtfully: 'Marty. Such a nice name...' implying this is the moment when she decides what they will name their future son. It is somewhat incongruous then, that their first born is called 'Dave'.

inference made could be correct and reliable, and contribute towards an accurate story understanding. However, in other cases, the inference may be misleading. As Bordwell observes:

> More often than we are usually aware, narratives invoke expectations only to defeat them, plan and time our encounters with information that will upset our assumptions, encourage us to extrapolate and then chide us for going too far, parade a host of positive instances before trotting out the single and crucial exception, hold back basic data while "prattling" (Barthes' term) about irrelevancies — all the while forcing us to keep to a predetermined temporal sequence and yoking us to a fixed rate of comprehension that makes us err simply by pressure of the clock. Narrative art ruthlessly exploits the tentative, probabilistic nature of mental activity (Bordwell, 1985b, p.39).

As discussed earlier, a story is a fiction, and the length of a story is largely a result of the author's duty to lead us a dance, not tell us the truth. Writers can use our tendency to pre-empt and predict to set the story framework. The key question dynamic discussed earlier is an example. In most cases, the protagonist's aim is accurately foreshadowed by the question raised (can Marty reunite his parents in love?), but the method by which he might achieve this is constantly thrown into doubt. However, in other cases, the audience may make interpretive errors, or the writer can deliberately misdirect the audience, enticing them to come to an assumed conclusion about future events or past foundations which turn out to be incorrect. In all these eventualities, a knowledge gap is set up between the hypothesis the perceiver has created for themselves and the actual direction the story is going to take. As Bordwell (1985b, p.39) adds, "a film may contain cues and structures that encourage the viewer to make errors of comprehension; in such cases, the film 'wants' a short- or long-term 'misunderstanding' ".

When Marty first arrives in 1955, he crashes into a barn on Peabody's Farm. As the farmer and his family cautiously approach the barn, they interpret the DeLorean as a spaceship and Marty, still dressed in his radiation suit and helmet, as an alien "mutating into human form" (Dialogue from *Back to the Future,* 1985). Peabody's son shows his family the cover of his 1950's sci-fi comic, which serves to confirm these misinterpretations. There is a knowledge gap between what the audience knows (the current truth of Marty's situation and why the Peabody's might understandably interpret his DeLorean as a spaceship), and the Peabody family's misinterpretation of that same situation from their perspective. This is a privilege class of misdirection whereby the audience knows that a character has made a misinterpretation and is misguided in the decisions they are making as a result, as distinct from a revelation class where it is the audience which is misled.

4.4.5.7 Knowledge Gaps through Suspense

Branigan, in his discussion of hierarchies of knowledge, investigated how Alfred Hitchcock created suspense:

> Using the example of a bomb placed in a briefcase under a table, he explained how he could create feelings of suspense, mystery, or surprise in the audience. If the spectator knows about the bomb, but not the characters seated around the table, then the spectator will be in suspense and must anxiously await the bomb's discovery or explosion (Branigan, 1992, p.75).

Thus, suspense is created using, once more, a difference in the knowledge held by different participants in the story. For the purposes of separating gap types, knowledge gaps through suspense are specifically recorded to account for those events in a narrative which are predictable, but not specific or guaranteed (otherwise the knowledge is already present and there is no gap). For example, if the audience is made aware of a bomb placed in a briefcase, the predictable outcome is that the bomb will, at some point, explode. However, knowledge gaps through suspense account for those events in which a promise of future relevant action is made, but without any foreshadowing of its form; the hermeneutic activities of the viewer simply have them open a gap in knowledge of a form that betrays their anxiety to know: 'What will happen next?'

As mentioned in the discussion of knowledge gaps through promise, everything within the mise-en-scène is there for a reason. Every item, character, object and event will contribute something to the narration's time, space or causal logic, and a receiver will always begin to wonder what the point of every object, action or character is as soon as it is brought to their attention, and this potential can readily be raised to become suspense. (More on this in a moment.)

In *Back to the Future*, following Marty's traumatic journey back to 1955, his escape from Peabody's Farm and the breakdown of the time machine, Marty walks towards Hill Valley for the first time as a member of the public in 1955. He is lost and alone, his parents and home are gone, his future is uncertain, and the non-specific question is raised in the minds of the audience: 'What will happen now?'

More orthodox forms of suspense are found in *The Big Sleep* (1946, Howard Hawkes). As the climax approaches, Marlowe organises for the mob boss, Eddie Mars, to meet him and Vivian at Geiger's house, tricking him into thinking he and Vivian must travel down from Realito. Marlowe knows Mars will rush up to the house with his henchmen to set an ambush, but Marlowe and Vivian are already at Geiger's house. As they prepare for Mars' arrival, Marlowe admits to Vivian that he is scared. They will be heavily outnumbered. This could be his dying hour. As Mars' inevitable arrival approaches the audience experiences a knowledge gap through suspense; what will happen when Mars and his heavies arrive?

Suspense also characterises a knowledge gap which is a function of a compound or complex question becoming reasserted by story events. Rather than asking the same question again, the suspense is inherent in the reminder that the knowledge gap is still open. In any event, a knowledge gap through suspense is the gap between a potential recognised in the situation as it stands and the inevitability of that potential being realised.

4.4.5.8 Knowledge Gaps through Distraction

Knowledge gaps through distraction occur when a character, whom the audience recognises will shortly suffer negative consequences, becomes entangled with irrelevances. The suspense and the resolution of existing open knowledge gaps is postponed as the character dallies at a time when the audience knows that urgent action is advisable. Little Red Riding Hood, on the advice of the wolf, spends time picking flowers as the wolf steals a march, eats her grandmother, dresses in Grandma's nightclothes and sets his trap for Little Red Riding Hood. A knowledge gap through distraction occurs when a character does not appreciate the full implications of some element of their life, and therefore happily indulges in activities which would not be of high priority if they fully understood their situation.

Knowledge gaps through distraction are closely related to suspense, in the sense that they are used to delay the delivery of knowledge and extend the period a gap remains open. They are both common mechanism for the writer looking to find compelling diversions for his audience whilst building a substantial plot.

In *Back to the Future*, when Marty is attempting to get George to ask Lorraine out, George is quite happy to give in to his reluctance and sit at home with his sci-fi television programmes and comics, rather than risking rejection by asking Lorraine to go out with him. Whilst George is happily looking to his hobby, the chances of his family existing in the future are reducing and he is unwittingly becoming responsible for Marty's death. This is a knowledge gap through distraction. Distractions of this nature serve not only to delay the resolution of existing knowledge gaps which are causing suspense, but also to introduce a gap between what the characters are concerned with and what the audience is anxiously urging them to prioritise more highly.

4.4.5.9 Knowledge Gaps through Mise-en-Scène

Knowledge can be held (and therefore withheld) by objects as well as by characters and events. For example, a card placed face-down on a poker table can withhold knowledge that can start a gun fight. A moving curtain, a hidden door, a wrapped present all hold and withhold information. As has been said, every object, character and event is likely to be meaningful to the overall story and the receiver will note and suspect everything to which their attention is drawn.

In *Some Like it Hot* (1959, directed by Billy Wilder) the coffin in the hearse is later found to contain hundreds of bottles of alcohol, so it is hiding information significant to the subterfuge of the funeral parlour as a façade for a party of illegal drinking. This is an example of a knowledge gap through mise-en-scène.

4.4.5.10 Knowledge Gaps through Comedy

Humour is highly subjective. However, it is exceptional in the sense that many humorous stories do not follow the canonical patterns of Hollywood narrative. As Steve Neale and Frank Krutnik (1990, p.30) point out, "comedy is often a generic exception to the rules and regimes of motivation that tend to govern most other Hollywood genres". Humour is afforded primacy over other contributing elements, and the narrative elements prescribed for other genres are of lesser consequence insofar as the work is funny enough.

However, within or outside of the classical Hollywood style, comedy makes use of knowledge gaps. To demonstrate this, and to create a framework in which to capture knowledge gaps through comedy, I will use two theories of humour (as discussed in detail by Adrian Bardon [2005]):

1. **Superiority Theory.** According to Bardon (2005. p.3), the superiority theory of comedy was first documented by Plato and Aristotle some 2,300 years ago. It holds that we find humour in the recognition of the downfall or inferiority of others, and we pleasure in the implicit superiority of ourselves. Hence, many favourite comic characters are inept, incompetent or foolish, from circus clowns and court jesters through to contemporary characters such as Basil Fawlty, Inspector Clouseau and, of course, Chaplin's Tramp. Thomas Hobbes further developed the theory in the 17th century, contending that "laughter is always antagonistic and conflictual, establishing a hierarchy at the moment of pleasure" (Stott, 2005, p.133).

   More recently, Charles Gruner has claimed that he can find superiority in all forms of humour: "Think of all humor as a succession of games. The very idea of a game implies fun [...]; but it also implies competition, keeping score and a winner and a loser" (Gruner, 1997, p.2). He also points out that superiority, that is, being a 'winner', does not necessarily have to involve a 'loser'. One can win freedom from bias or prejudice or get married and feel good about that without putting someone else down, and this slightly broader interpretation of the term 'superiority' gives the theory greater completeness (Gruner, 1997, p.8). According to Gruner, good humour comes from "'winning' [...] in its broadest sense: 'Getting what you want' makes us happy [...and...] getting what we want suddenly, as a surprise, exhilarates us far more than receiving the same thing as a matter of course" (ibid.). It is this which is the cause of laughter. He further claims that "with humor, our behaviour indicating pleasure (usually laughing, smiling, grinning, sometimes screaming with joy or applause) varies with [...] the abruptness or suddenness of the surprising outcome" (ibid.).

Many disagree with Gruner's blanket approach. Bardon (2005, p.5) explains that given examples in which humour exists where no superiority is involved, in the case of puns, riddles or humorous images, caused philosophers, such as Francis Hutcheson, Immanuel Kant, Arthur Schopenhauer and Søren Kierkegaard, to embrace and advance the **incongruity theory**.

2. **Incongruity Theory** holds that humour is found primarily in a recognition of "an incongruity between expectation and reality [...] some sort of unusual or unexpected juxtaposition of events, objects, or ideas" (Bardon, 2005, p.6). For example, in the joke, 'there are two fish in a tank. One says to the other, 'do you know how to drive this thing?' The incongruity is present in the difference between the expectation created by the first sentence (an image of two fish in an aquarium) and the ultimate meaning established by the end (an image of two fish finding themselves in charge of a military tank).

Although the incongruity is evident, Gruner argues that such humour remains in the domain of superiority theory; it is only the focus of superiority that has moved. Humour of this form, which includes puns, riddles and verbal ingenuity, carries implicit superiority in the cleverness of the authors as they (at least temporarily) "'defeat' their targets/public with brilliant verbal exhibitionism" (Gruner, 1997, p.145).

Knowledge Gaps in Humour Theories
These two principal theories, incongruity and superiority, have been used to capture the humour in my case studies. It is acknowledged that they may not capture all humour for all spectators. Nonetheless, this is not the aim of the research, and these theories do provide reasonable and manifest indicators

of the presence of humour. In both theories, there is a gap in knowledge that signals the presence of humour between the 'knowing' superior and the ignorant inferior in superiority theory or between what was expected and what actually happens in the case of incongruity. In either case, a knowledge gap is implicit whereby a scenario is deliberately built in one direction and then paid-off in another. The setup creates a knowledge gap between the implied and the actual situation. The sudden pleasure of understanding that comes in the switch from one to the other is the cause of the laughter.

A knowledge gap through comedy is recorded when there is:

a) A tangible switch from an expectation set to either a new superiority dynamic, or

b) A tangible switch from an expectation to an incongruous outcome.

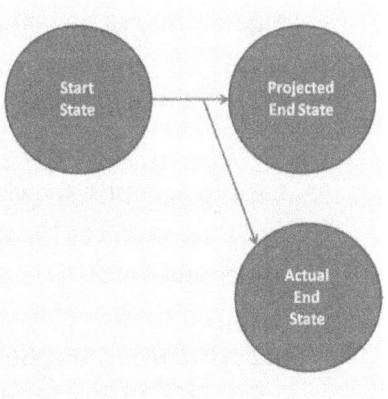

An example of both these dynamics is found in *Some Like it Hot* (1959). When Gerry and Joe (Jack Lemmon and Tony Curtis), masquerading as the female band members, Daphne and Josephine, arrive at the hotel with the other members of the band, they are competing to impress the attractive lead singer, Sugar Kane (Marilyn Monroe). Jerry offers to carry Sugar's bags and musical equipment. This is incongruous behaviour for one woman towards another and the audience knows that Daphne is really a man trying to be chivalrous. Joe, as Josephine, sees the pointlessness of chivalry between women, thanks Daphne warmly and loads her up with 'her' bags and musical equipment as well, asserting a superiority over Jerry in their competition for Sugar's affections on top of the incongruity as Joe links arms with Sugar and they stroll unencumbered into the hotel. It is measurable incongruity and superiority of this type which characterises knowledge gaps through comedy.

It is acknowledged that mechanisms of comedy could extend beyond these epistemological boundaries, and that not all humour for all spectators can be captured. However, these mechanisms cover the majority of cases in current theories of humour and provide an objective basis for a knowledge gap theory which accounts for humour in a story.

4.4.5.11 Knowledge gaps through Aristotle Principles

In his *Poetics* (Aristotle, 335BC [1996]) Aristotle outlines three aspects of a story, each of which carries a form of knowledge gap:

1. **The harmatia** ('mistake') is an event in the story which throws the protagonist's world out of balance, raising questions in the mind of the audience: 'What is going to happen?' 'How will this be fixed?' These questions are gaps in knowledge. Thus, in *Back to the Future* George McFly's world is thrown out of balance when he tears open the car door to role play his fight with Marty only to find Biff is sitting in the car instead of Marty.

2. **The anagnorisis** ('realisation') is the moment in a narrative when the truth of the situation is recognised by the protagonist. It usually heralds a need for the protagonists to dig much deeper if a positive outcome is to be achieved. A gap in the protagonist's knowledge must first be present before a truth can dawn and the story is, therefore, progressed through a knowledge gap.

   In *Back to the Future*, George McFly's anagnorisis comes when he realises that if he does not stand and fight his feared nemesis, Biff, he will be leaving Lorraine to be abused by Biff in the car. The power of the realisation is that it is a choice of evils for George. Stand and fight (and risk a beating) or run away as he would prefer (and leave Lorraine to be abused).

   There may be more than one realisation in a story, but Aristotle (335BC [1996]) asserted that anagnorisis is causally linked to a peripeteia (a reversal of fortunes at the finale, discussed next). Realisation can also occur for other participants; it can occur too late to allow remedial action, or it can occur after the peripeteia (as is often the case in a Greek tragedy). In

Shakespeare's *Romeo and Juliet*, the audience realises the series of events that are leading inexorably to their deaths whereas Romeo and Juliet never find out the truth.

3. **The peripeteia** ('reversal') is a reversal or twist in expectation. As a story event approaches its climax the audience has generally been given strong expectations as to what will happen. The peripeteia is the twist in expectation for the audience in this context. George's realisation that he must stand and fight Biff or leave Lorraine to be abused in the car leads to a peripeteia twist in the form of a third option that was not foreseen. Rather than get a beating or let Lorraine suffer, George stands his ground and manages to defeat the bully. This peripeteia causes two major plot reversals. Firstly, George and Marty's plan achieves its outcome. Even though it went disastrously wrong, Lorraine now finds George attractive even though he is being true to himself (such that they did not need a role play to trick Lorraine into finding him attractive); secondly, the marked increase in quality evident in Marty's 1985 family and lifestyle as a result of George having been strong and assertive for the intervening 30 years.

In another example, when Marty returns to 1985, he uses the time machine to give himself an extra ten minutes to save Doc Brown's life from the terrorist shooting. However, this is not enough time. He arrives in 1985 in a different part of town and is obliged to use that time up trying to get back to the car park in which Doc Brown was gunned down. Marty's anagnorisis (realisation) comes when he realises that he is too late. He had a time machine. He could easily have prevented this tragedy, but he failed to give himself enough time and Doc is gunned down. The realisation hits Marty hard. He has made a terrible mistake. However, the peripeteia comes when Doc Brown sits up. He is alive. Doc Brown did heed the warning from 1955 and was wearing a bullet-proof vest when the attack happened.

The anagnorisis is a knowledge gap between what the protagonist knew before the realisation, and what he knows that causes the realisation. The peripeteia is a knowledge gap between what the audience has been given to expect will happen and what does happen as a result of the twist in expectation.

Note that although I listed all Aristotle's principles together in this section, the peripeteia and some forms of anagnorisis are knowledge gaps through storification.

4.4.6 Knowledge Gaps through Storification

Section 1 built upon Barthes' (1990, pp.4-8) concept of narration as a "galaxy of signifiers [...] forming 'nebulae' of signifieds", adding a diachronic dimension to assert narrative events (the narrafication of the sign) and from there, adding human interpretation and receiver knowledge to create meta-meaning in mind from assimilating all these dynamics; for example, the moral message in a children's story is not stated in the narration, but is a meaning created in mind by the receiver as a result of receiving the narration. The establishment of meaning in mind from receiving a narration is what I have termed the storification of the sign.

The storification category of knowledge gap requires a receiver with the appropriate personal knowledge and history to project into the gaps and complete the causal logic not just of significations, but of linked events — narrafications.

Think of a piece of iron ore in a hillside. It's a signifier. Once it is formed into a thing we culturally recognise as a 'bullet', now, for those who know what a bullet is and what it does, it is a signification. Once it is used in a gun to shoot at another human being, this is a narrafication. Seeing a person with a rifle on their back and recognising the potential to be shot is storification. Making human sense of the narrative implicit to the conditions and objects (gun, bullet, soldier, environment...) and the way they may come together in a narrative is storification. And supreme storification occurs once one takes the significance of these bullets and joins them into a bigger picture involving war, politics and propaganda, morality and ideology. Cultural elements that require significant knowledge to understand as they create sense from conjoining many narrative objects and cultural understanding that are already in themselves storifications. Where it has been asserted several times in this work that there is no truth in story, only meaning, storification is the personal mental process of deriving meaning in mind from receiving a narration.

In one sense, a storification is to a narrafication what a signification is to a sign. The upgrade is, however, dimensionally more substantial. A storification is not simply an enormous number of signs coming at you in a machine-gun series. A storification must include the social significance of the relationships between events and the objects they contain. However, once a person is knowledgeable, in the sense that they 'get' the storification from the narrative, it is unconscious and automatic. In the same way that a rose instantly becomes a signification for a person with the cultural knowledge of romance and courtship, so the presence of a bullet instantly and unconsciously storifies into an event involving shooting.

It is hard to overstate the importance of the storification dynamic. If a receiver of a sign (say, a gun) is oblivious to the cultural imperatives that cause the signification (death), the signification (and therefore the *significance*) is non-existent. If the receiver is oblivious to the cultural imperatives inherent in a narrative event, the storification is non-existent, which is why a deer will wander towards a gun pointed at it and sniff the muzzle with curiosity. When the wolf invites Little Red Riding Hood to enjoy the woodland and pick some flowers to take to her grandmother, there is a narrative logic that is understood. Human beings pick flowers, join them together into aesthetically pleasing groups and give them to each other to bring pleasure and consolidate relationships. Understanding this is a narrafication with elements of storification (the cultural components of friendship involving flowers). However, for those with appropriate cultural understanding, the event involving a girl picking flowers includes a further storification that overwhelms the innocent interpretation for those who understand the inherent danger in a predatory animal. There is a narrative logic in the wolf going ahead to the grandmother's house. Joining these two narrafications/storifications together creates a further storification that makes the story gripping and powerful. It is engaging because we make those meta-connections for ourselves and produce the story in mind for ourselves.

It is at this meta-level of significations, joined into storifications, built into wider storifications that sophisticated and complex stories are built.

If the writerly work of the receiver of a narration is critical to the definitive presence of a story (and I argue that it is), then suffice to say that the storification category of knowledge gaps is *exclusively* dependent upon the receiver's personal mental input. If a receiver of a narrafication is oblivious to the cultural imperatives that cause the storification, the storification (and therefore the story) is non-existent. Storification gaps are often contrived entirely in mind, combining internally-contrived knowledge with other internally-contrived knowledge to create the logic and subtext which goes into the storification gaps. If you consider how the moral message of a children's story arrives in mind, it is generally entirely through the work of the receiver. The message implicit to *Little Red Riding Hood*, that a child should not talk to strangers, is not stated by the characters or in the storyline. It is divined in abstract thought through receiving the narration and overlaying cultural knowledge on the events.

Storification is also predominantly a part of the *outcome* of a series of linked events. indeed, it is not possible to form a storification gap without going through the gears of lower level story dynamics from the mimetic and orientating categories that create the conditions required for a storification. If a narration has a beginning, a middle and an end, the aim of the lower phases is to create the conditions that can deliver a story (storification) that is greater than the sum of its parts (narrafications). Storifications are, to a large extent, the ultimate deliverable in a successful story; the defining triumph that everything else in the story has been building towards. Although it is not an axiomatic requirement for a story to have storification gaps — indeed, it is perfectly possible to have a story without one — in my research, all of the most highly rated stories have storifications that are a requirement of comprehending the narration in the way that is apparently intended. Indeed, *The Big Sleep* provides a strong indication of the power of storification. It is a story with a confusing and evidently unsatisfactory narrative. However, the storification gaps are strong and clear — and the story is a recognised classic (IMDB, 2018; BFI, 2012). More on storification in *The Big Sleep* later, however, I argue that its success is because the storifications are the most important factor in our appreciation of a narration.

4.4.6.1 Quality of Life

That last paragraph is one of many moments in this work where the assertion of subjective values is required to discuss or demonstrate a story's 'quality' or a character's situation, change, personal growth or motivation. For story quality, I use the hundreds-of-thousands of public ratings for each film on the internet movie database (IMDB, 2018) and the BFI decennial poll of critics and directors for the greatest films of all time (BFI, 2012) to work for me effectively as a survey. However, character values and 'quality of life' are subjective areas that are challenging to define appropriately. Maslow's 'Hierarchy of Needs' (Maslow, 1954, p.236) provides a useful illustration to exemplify a set of life values which can be applied in the classification of knowledge gaps which depend upon a measure of change, growth and motivation.

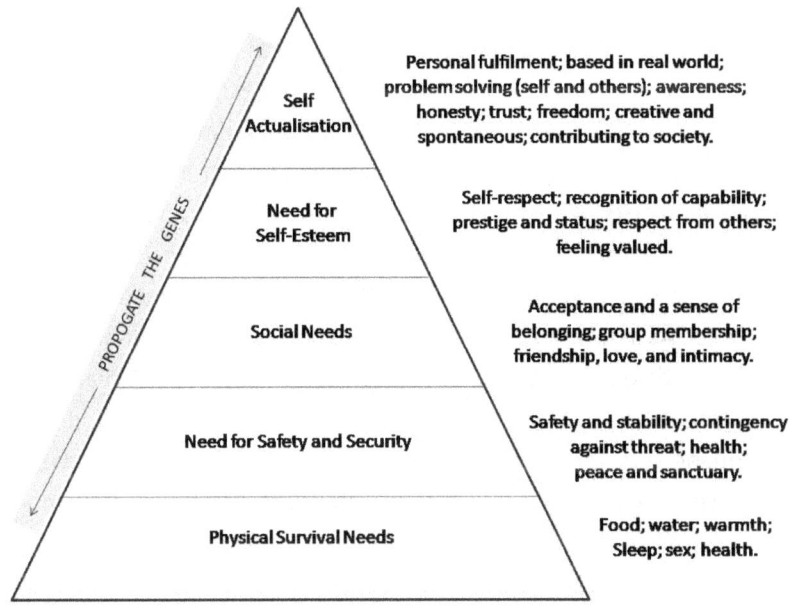

Figure 14 - Maslow's Hierarchy of Needs (Maslow, 1954)

Maslow's (1954) hierarchy does not provide for all possible learning and growth, but it is used here for its value in providing indicative reference for step changes in life values or relative quality of life.

In a fairy tale, the brave knight does not simply slay the dragon. He changes his life values, ending the story with a castle, a kingdom and the hand of a princess in marriage *as a result* of being brave and slaying a dragon. The story world does not change across the arc (although it might have done); it was the knight whose quality of life changed within that world. While structuralists focus on the clear and measurable defeat of the dragon (the denoted structural element within the narrafication), it is the more subtle 'life value' dynamics — the implications in life and morality for the characters — which this research seeks to exploit. The holes, not the net. Although life values are subjective, Maslow's hierarchy can help us to illustrate a change in life values as a representation for what happens in the story that gives it more grip than the evident protagonist victory over a dragon. The latter is the narrafication; assimilating and understanding the changes in life values that the narrafication facilitates for the knight is storification.

The structuralist recognises the symbolic objects of pain or pleasure (dragon, death, castle, kingdom, gold, hand in marriage...) and tracks them as indicators of success and failure, and even uses them to indicate, through acquisition or loss, the presence of character growth in a story. However, these are elements of the narrafication. They are identifiable facets in the information stream, not in knowledge and meaning. In *Back to the Future*, a Toyota pickup truck is presented as the symbol of aspiration and success for Marty McFly. As a new Toyota pickup is transported around the square, Marty watches it with desire: "Some day, Jennifer... Some day..." (dialogue from *Back to the Future*, 1985). Ultimately, after the climax and during the resolution, he gets one, and this is, for the structuralist, a box ticked, because it symbolises Marty's character growth. However, Marty was only indirectly responsible for gaining this symbol of success. In reality, his dad bought it for him. In the real world, if a dad buys a car for his son, this is not a cultural indicator that the son is in any way brave or worthy, so marking this acquisition as of structural significance is, at best, of indirect value. The true character growth that leads to this acquisition is undergone by George McFly. George is the one who changes, and learns, and grows, through the decisions he makes under pressure. George takes a moral stance, despite the danger to himself. Through standing up to both the bully, Biff, and overcoming his own insecurities he gains the courage of his convictions. He grows as a person.

Sure, this brings him riches and Lorraine's hand in marriage but these outcomes are not the engaging power-base of the story. These are symbols of George's success that arrive as a *consequence* of his character growth. Analysis that identifies the 'knowledge growth' of a character at the time it happens rather than the symbolic change in their environment or circumstances more accurately captures the narration's power-base for engagement.

Marty's acquisition of the pickup truck, flagged as aspiration at the beginning and delivered as a symbol of success at the end, is a fine example of the inaccuracy inherent in structuralism. It notices the denoted symbol of Marty's 'success' but is disconnected from the source of this gain for Marty in the true power of the story: George's change in life values achieved through making decisions under pressure causing personal learning and growth. We in the audience understand that George's decision under pressure led to the positive outcome he gets. The meaning that emerges into our mind, perhaps that it is necessary to have the courage of one's convictions to lead a fulfilling life, is a storification.

As we shall see in the listing of storification gap types (coming next), a knowledge gap approach captures these life-value dynamics, even though they are based on subjective values — that which is not present — and a need for receiver writerly work to be done before a tangible element manifests. This is a significant difference from a structuralist approach.

Storification gaps draw subtext from the receiver. If a denoted sign is the physical netting, and the significations are the constitutive absence (the holes in the net) which make the net meaningful, then the narrafications are a fishing boat and storification is the human meaning of it all; the nourishment in a beautifully cooked tuna ready on the plate back home. Storifications are the deeply meaningful point of the whole thing. The net may have been important, and yes, understanding the design and the narrative mechanics of the net and the reason for the boat are all useful and necessary to narrative construction... but the real meaning is nothing to do with practicalities, and all to do with human meaning.

I argue that contemporary script guidance rarely addresses subtext at any level because it is not amenable to deconstruction. It is too abstract; a quality rather than a structural element. A structuralist can point at the pickup truck, and can identify a turning point when George wins the conflict with Biff, but it cannot identify George's moral growth and learning. Storification is a complex component of the phenomenology — the knowledge stream and human causal logic in mind — and that is what must be captured.

This is a critical benefit of a knowledge gap approach. Whilst structural imperatives can be seen to have a knowledge gap at the root, the reverse is not true. A key question, for example, is a structural element, evident within the text, and is also a knowledge gap (there is always a gap in knowledge between a question and its answer). However, not all knowledge gaps convert readily into structural elements. However, a storification — say, a moral message in a story — must be derived in mind by the receiver and formulated from the causal logic in mind. It is a knowledge gap between the understanding of the course of events in the narrafication (what happens) and the establishment of the meta-meaning (the moral understanding in the mind of the receiver — what it *means*) once the writerly work has been done. The storification does not have a tangible presence in the text. It must be thought into being and exists only in the mind of the receiver. It is at this point that structuralist theories break down and a knowledge gap approach comes into its own. Subtext can be defined in knowledge gap terms: Subtext is the knowledge that goes into the gap between what is stated and what is understood. Storification dynamics are clearly composed of knowledge gaps and yet are challenging to frame in structural terms. (Unless, of course, we create a structuralist model from the system of (the language of) knowledge gaps. We then get the best of both worlds. More on this shortly.)

For the moment, then, storification gaps are challenging to capture because they are empirically vague. They are the extreme example of how the constitutive absence of gaps is the defining substance of a story. I will use Maslow's hierarchy of need as a measure for changes in subjective values concerned with a character's fortunes, values and quality of life.

4.4.6.2 Knowledge gaps through Character Growth

Character growth is a significant positive or negative change in the quality and values of a character's life that is a result of the character's experiences and is evidenced by the actions they take and consequences of those actions. Note that the actions do not themselves demonstrate the growth; it is the change in actions across the course of the character's experience that represents the growth. The change in mindset causes a different action due to learning. This change in mindset is the growth, and the actions consequent to that change create the evidential gap that is filled (explained) by the change in mindset. In *The Big Sleep*, Marlowe changes his mindset from a rigid assertion of the rule of law to the assertion of a morality of which he approved, but which was, strictly speaking, illegal. The differences between the actions he took towards criminals through the body of the story (asserting the letter of the law) and the actions he took towards criminals (Vivian and her sister, Carmen) later in the story when the pressure was on him to assert the law, evidenced the change in his mindset (his character has grown). He applied compassion and his own moral values instead of the law; indeed, through this character growth and the decisions to which it led, he became a criminal himself, however, we in the audience understood that the morality applied was, in this case, finer than that enshrined in law. (I go through the storification of *The Big Sleep* in detail shortly.)

Character growth is a gap in knowledge between the life values of a character at the outset and the life values of a character as a result of their experiences and the consequences of the decisions or actions they take in the narration. The knowledge that goes into that gap is the audience understanding of what the character learned because the actions they took had outcomes that can be seen as a tangible cost or benefit in their life.

The outcome of *Back to the Future* is directly dependent upon George learning a life lesson and, as a result of that learning, using that knowledge to improve his quality of life. George McFly is, for the majority of the story, weak and unassertive. This is an internal conflict, because he does not wish to behave in the ways he does. He is too weak to behave in the ways he would choose for himself were he brave enough to be true to himself. He avoids confrontation and runs away from difficult decisions until events conspire to force him to confront his internal conflict. In the pivotal scene, George McFly, racked with self-doubt and lacking assertiveness, stumbles across his nemesis, the muscle-bound bully, Biff, in the act of abusing Lorraine in a parked car. The scene forces George to confront his own weakness by offering him a choice of evils. He can stand and fight and risk a beating from the bully or turn and run, as he usually would, and leave Lorraine to be abused. Unable to simply run away from confrontation or to contemplate leaving Lorraine in this situation, he makes a fist and takes Biff on. George wins the fight. In doing so, in that moment under pressure, he demonstrates to himself that he can be assertive. He learns to have the courage of his convictions and, with this change in mindset, his character grows. Because his self-doubts are gone, his confidence and strength then pervade everything in his life. George changed and he learned, and that growth had a direct impact on the story outcomes.

As with any gaps, it is left to the receiver to provide the knowledge that goes in to the gap and interpret the consequences of George's actions. For some, the change from running away to standing his ground demonstrates firstly that George has overcome his weakness, and secondly, a morality that can be related to the real world: a person must have the courage of their convictions to lead a fulfilling life.

As with all knowledge gaps, some may not get any such subtext. For example, the scene also presents a dynamic that shows George proving his worth in masculine and perhaps anachronistic ways, protecting a woman through male violence. Some may find this offensive while others may experience a different interpretation. As already stated, it is not my role to judge or specify the fabula for an individual spectator. However, in the exemplified or an equivalent way, a knowledge gap can be found in the lesson that is taught or learned through the experiences of a character in a story. I do not need to state the mindset or interpretation of the receiver, what I need to do is identify the gap, and that is readily apparent in the unexpected choice George makes and the outcome he gets.

This said, the story arc demonstrated by George McFly is common in highly rated stories. Aristotle based his philosophical investigations in *Ethics* on the question: How should a human being lead their life? Addressing this question is fundamental to every human being, and is therefore, often at the core of stories which become popular, because people thirst for knowledge and crave understanding-through-narrative for themselves in their own journey. When the question of how a person should lead their life is addressed in a story, it is answered through the differences between a character's life values, self-knowledge and personal circumstances at the beginning of the film and those at the end. The changes take place through the decisions the characters make and the experiences they have because of those decisions.

In *Some Like it Hot*, Joe (Tony Curtis) finds Sugar (Marilyn Monroe) highly attractive. He devotes himself to tricking her into having sex with him. However, in the end he is uncovered as a licentious trickster and fraud and is forced to reveal his true self. It is at this point that their relationship truly blossoms. He learns (and therefore teaches a receiver) that relationships built on deception and lies are less fulfilling than those built on trust and respect. He takes this learning forwards into his life with Sugar Kane. On the other hand, Jerry (Jack Lemmon) learns to accept the love of another man and move on from the strident assertion of his heterosexual values. The audience might learn from the story that alternative gender constructs are acceptable in life, and people should not be judged or persecuted for their sexuality or gender preferences.

Character growth is the storification that is most commonly found in the most highly rated stories, specifically when that character growth is a function of moral learning, and that learning is applied by the character in their behaviours and therefore drives the resolution of the story's key conflicts.

4.4.6.3 Knowledge Gaps through Vicarious Learning

One of the highest functions of storification is the possibility for a lesson learned by a character (or failed to be learned by a character) To influence a receiver's perspective on the real world. Much of the time, a storification teaches a lesson to a receiver that is taken on board as a form of meaning that does not influence the receiver's own values and behaviours. For example, the knowledge that there is a chap called Santa Claus who lives at the North Pole, judges us on good and bad behaviour, and delivers toys on Christmas eve is a fiction, but it has meaning that is taken forwards, and has a significant impact on a receiver's life and behaviours. The knowledge that a wolf might trick you, eat your grandmother and then eat you is a fiction that — whilst not making a receiver fearful of cross-dressing wolves — is pattern-matched against real-world understanding and potentially delivers great impact on the values, morality and behaviours of individuals and the way they react towards strangers in the real world. All of these are knowledge gaps through vicarious learning, whereby the learning is not confined to the story and its literal interpretation but reaches into the mindset of the receiver in ways that extend into their life beyond the end of the reception of a narration.

George McFly's decision to stand up to the bully led to his positive character growth, and lessons could be learned (knowledge gaps filled) from the story events surrounding his decisions. Different spectators might come to different conclusions, and because the fabula cannot be specified, and neither can an individual's personal fabula, so we can never say who learned what, but the denoted presence of character actions which lead to a significantly positive or negative outcome is a knowledge gap through vicarious learning that, it is reasonable to assert, will cue a learning response from a spectator. The gap is there, so knowledge (subtext) will be the outcome. Sometimes the resultant story will include new learning, and some of that might be genuinely applicable to a fulfilling life in the real world.

4.4.6.4 Knowledge Gaps through Surpassing Aim

By the end of a story, the protagonist may have gained more than they set out to achieve or gained something different from that which they set out for, and they may have changed or grown as a person due to their experiences. The protagonist might set out with a clear aim. However, when they reach the point where they can achieve their goals, their experiences have changed their values; that is, they have learned and grown, and they forgo these rewards for some finer surpassing aim they initially did not aspire to or value as highly as the original aim.

An example of this dynamic is found in *It's a Wonderful Life* (1946, directed by Frank Capra). George Bailey's (James Stewart) clear and stated aim is to make a million dollars. By the end of the film he fails to achieve this but realises he is "the richest man in Bedford Falls" because he has a wonderful family, and he is loved and respected by the community he now values and of which he feels proud to be a part. The message is that these are greater riches than the million dollars he perceived was of ultimate value at the start. He did not achieve his aim, but his learning through his actions and the changes in his priorities meant he achieved something more — a surpassing aim. More than just money; and more than just the riches of a family and community; he found in himself the ability to recognise, value and appreciate family and community for their true worth.

In *Back to the Future* Marty McFly's aim is to get back to 1985. He achieves his aim, but in doing so he also managed to improve his father's strength of character and therefore the quality of life for his entire family as a result of his actions. This was an aim he did not even realise he aspired to at the outset.

A knowledge gap of this type happens when a protagonist has demonstrated clear aims, the achievement of which define the story. However, by the end of the story, the protagonist has gained something different, and subjectively finer, than that which they set out for. This knowledge gap dynamic is documented as a knowledge gap through surpassing aim. The actions and outcomes may be implicitly supportive or subversive towards the dominant ideology, but the dynamic demonstrates the action of knowledge gaps through storification that can potentially influence a spectator's cultural and political viewpoint.

4.4.6.5   Knowledge Gaps through Moral Argument

Morality is a difficult and subjective area for academic investigation. For exemplification purposes, it is fair to say that there may be a gap between a receiver's moral understanding (or even their moral stance) at the beginning of a story and the end. In a story such as *Little Red Riding Hood*, a receiver may emerge from the story feeling that it is wise for young children not to talk to strangers. The story is a moral argument that strongly asserts this mantra — this 'side' of the moral argument.

Almost all stories can be viewed through a moral lens, and a knowledge gap found as a result. However, because the initial moral stance and the possible consequential moral stance involve purely subjective assertion with regard to the thoughts and feelings of the receiver.

4.4.6.6   Knowledge Gaps through Metaphor and Allegory

A metaphor links two disparate objects or concepts by overlaying the qualities of one on to the other in order to rhetorically enhance the meaning of the latter. Shakespeare, for example has Romeo use metaphor to explain his feelings about Juliet: "But soft! What light through yonder window breaks? It is the east, and Juliet, the sun!" (William Shakespeare, *Romeo and Juliet*).

The two components of metaphor are known as the tenor (the original concept or object, in our case, Juliet) and the vehicle (the quality or concept overlaying the tenor to enhance its meaning — in this case, the rising sun). The overall effect is to provide a single metaphor: the combined image of Juliet imagined as the miracle wonder of the rising sun in human form.

There is an implicit knowledge gap between the tenor and the full final metaphor. A gap filled by information concerning the vehicle drawn from the receiver's history and experience. By understanding how much we have loved the glorious, awakening effect of a sunrise in our own lives, we understand the effect the appearance of Juliet has on Romeo. In this way, every metaphor can be seen to be a storification gap. The fabula created in mind implicitly includes cultural understanding of vehicle material which is not explicitly stated in the narration, relying on the spectators' history and experience to generate not only the knowledge that fills the gap but also adding together the sum of the parts (the tenor and the vehicle) to complete the metaphor. The strategy of extending a metaphor through an entire narrative so that objects, persons, and actions in the text are equated with meanings that lie outside the text creates an allegory.

To put it more simply, the knowledge gap is in the difference between the denoted information in the narration (tenor) and the interpreted knowledge in the created fabula (metaphor completed through the overlay of vehicle attributes). Of course, there are many metaphoric possibilities in a story; indeed, every story is essentially a representation that could be considered to be a metaphor. In *Modern Times*, an example of a metaphor occurs when the diegesis shows a mass of manual workers and people looking for work flocking to a factory entrance in the morning (tenor). The narration cuts to a flock of sheep (vehicle) being herded along a narrow path towards a fate that they do not control. Although we have no way of specifying a general audience response and cannot say with certainty that political messages are delivered, these possibilities demonstrate the function of a knowledge gap through metaphor/allegory.

4.4.6.7 Knowledge Gaps through Recognition and Allusion

In the context of Sternberg's narrative self-consciousness (as discussed in **section 4.4.3.2 — Knowledge gaps through Self-Conscious Narrator**) it is possible for the narration to communicate with the audience without the characters knowing of this collusion, thereby introducing a gap in knowledge between what the audience and the characters know. When Biff and George reprise their scene in 1955 whereby the bully, Biff, demands to know when George will do his homework for him, the audience *recognises* that this behaviour is a repeat of an interaction already viewed in earlier scenes, whilst Biff and George are not aware of the allusion.

Other examples include cultural references to objects and events in the real world, references that would not resonate with characters within the diegesis but will have significance for the audience. For example, in 1955, when Marty plays the song, *Johnny B Goode* (Berry, Chess Records, 1958) three years before Chuck Berry wrote it, audience members with appropriate cultural knowledge and history will understand the reference (and the suggestion that Marty's actions in 1955 might be responsible for originating the rock and roll phenomenon). The knowledge gap lies between the information that is available to the characters in their story world and the information that is available to the audience, given their cultural knowledge and experience.

A Storification Example

To complete the section on storification, I would like to exemplify just how important storification is to the overall power of a story using *The Big Sleep*. From a structural viewpoint, the inciting incident occurs in the first sequence when General Sternwood engages private detective Marlowe to work for him. The key question is raised: Will Marlowe solve the crime and rid the Sternwoods of their blackmailer?

The story builds a complex web of relationships, blackmail and criminal activity, including seven murders. The plot is notoriously confusing and the outcome uncertain. One of the best-known Hollywood anecdotes concerns the film's perplexing plot and is recalled by Lauren Bacall: "One day, Bogie [Humphrey Bogart] came on the set and said to Howard [Hawks, the director],

'Who pushed Taylor off the pier?' Everything stopped. Hawks sent Raymond Chandler a telegram asking whether the Sternwood's chauffeur, Owen Taylor, was murdered or if it was a suicide. 'Dammit I didn't know either,' Chandler recalled." (Ebert, 2012, p.27).

In addressing the plot confusion, Roger Ebert (1997, p.7) called it a story 'about the process of a criminal investigation, not its results'. The lack of logical closure to some plot lines and the confusing events of the story undermine the structural imperatives of most modern script consultants (specifically, McKee, [1998], Field, [1979] and King, [2001]), as well as working against the imperatives of classical Hollywood structure. For these theorists, a causal logic linking the climax and resolution to the events in the body of the story are vital to a story's success. *The Big Sleep* has an unresolved ending and yet is one of the most successful films of all time. When asked about it, the director Howard Hawks said there had been a lesson in the film about not needing to make sense; stating that it was more about having a 'good scene' or something that was 'fun', and carrying the audience along with you, scene by scene rather than ensuring a tight plot (Thomson, 1997, p. 63).

Clearly, the story gurus and creative professionals do not agree an explanation on how the film can be simultaneously confusing and highly rated. I agree with Hawks, but I do not believe he has the right interpretation. Every scene can be 'good' and 'fun' in the sense that the ample presence of knowledge gaps (and there are hundreds of them in *The Big Sleep*, many unresolved) demonstrates how an event can engage if it has knowledge gaps even in the absence of traditional structural imperatives. However, I argue that the reason the overall story is so very highly rated is to do with the substantive presence of the storification classification of knowledge gap types; and these storification gaps do all achieve satisfactory closure.

In knowledge gap terms, the most pervasive and durable knowledge gap lies in the choice Marlowe has to make between allowing himself to develop a relationship with Vivian Sternwood even though she is a suspect or asserting the law without question and ruining the possibility of finding love with Vivian. A receiver will know that Marlowe effectively personalises an institutional conflict, however he appears to suffer no conflict. He chooses to assert the letter of the law rigidly and without compromise at every opportunity. It is the only way to be clear and certain in the corrupt underbelly of society at that time. However, Vivian's situation makes his disciplined and unwavering approach to decision-making more difficult. It later transpires that she is a criminal. In the end, Marlowe must make a difficult choice. He finds the law, if asserted without question, will not provide justice, because Vivian is breaking the law in attempting to protect her younger sister from the mob. Vivian has broken the law but has done so because she is being wronged. So Marlowe asserts his own morality. He brings the criminal Eddie Mars to justice, killing him in the climax scene. He then does not hand Vivian over to the police, preferring to pin her crimes on Mars, who was the true bad guy and can no longer speak against her. As receivers, we can see that Marlowe has changed and grown, and applied that learning to his personal growth in order to assert moral values that are better than the law he so rigidly and unwaveringly applied before this difficult choice. This is a beautiful example of a storification gap — the gap between Marlowe's knowledge and motivation at the beginning of the story and his changed values driving the climax and resolution which defines *The Big Sleep*.

The plot is confusing and the outcome uncertain, however, I assert that the clear presence of strong storification gaps is of paramount importance in a receiver's appreciation of a story. It is the storification dynamics that distinguish the more highly regarded stories rather than the much-vaunted structural imperatives.

5 Case Study Recommendations

This section aims to demonstrate how the above information can be used in, for example, a close reading of a work of literature or a content analysis of a film story. A complete set of four case studies (*Modern Times* [Chaplin, 1936]; *The Big Sleep* [Hawks, 1946]; *Some Like it Hot* [Wilder, 1959] and *Back to the Future* [Zemekis, 1985]) were a part of my formal research on which this book is based. This research is available under separate cover, and includes access to the complete case studies, the data capture and the spreadsheets. The thesis document is entitled *Knowledge gaps in popular Hollywood cinema storytelling: The role of information disparity in film narrative* (Baboulene, 2017). This is also available commercially as an eBook.

For the purposes of this publication, I intended to provide an extract from the case study data capture. However, because it is in spreadsheet form and is difficult to display readably in book form, I have made a copy of the full spreadsheet freely available at my website:

www.baboulene.com/clipsanddata

Method

The analyst steps through the narration moment-by-moment identifying empirical differences in the knowledge held by different participants in the story. Each gap is documented in a row entry in the spreadsheet. The columns I used are as follows:

- **The Story Event.** A description of the action in which the knowledge gap is found.
- **The Knowledge Gap.** A description of the gap in the context of two participants.
- **Classification.** Whether the gap is privilege, revelation or ellipsis.
- **Category.** Whether the gap is paratext, orientating (diegetic), orientating (mimetic), mimetic or storification.
- **Type.** Identifies the gap type (see the complete list explained in depth through section 4).
- **Signified.** A short explanation of the human meaning or causal logic that makes the gap significant to the *knowledge* context.

- **Composition.** Whether the gap is simple, compound or complex in composition.

I also included a 'notes' column which I used for any additional explanation of the gap. Of course, you may list whichever columns work for you given the aims of your research.

It is also worth noting that a significant number of gaps, particularly the paratext and storification gaps, are not situated against a moment in the narration, so were listed in their own sections towards the beginning of the spreadsheet and again at the end, depending upon their chronological position. So, for example, the paratext associated with the star image of the main actors is generally present before the receiver enters the diegesis, so is listed in the first part of the spreadsheet. The moral message of a story is a storification gap discovered in the later stages and is therefore listed at the end of the spreadsheet.

If you are interested in carrying out a content analysis of this nature, do please feel free to download my full spreadsheet at:

www.baboulene.com/clipsanddata

5.1 Knowledge Gaps and Wider Applications

One of the most significant potential properties of a 'language of' knowledge gaps is a unification effect. The terms story, narrative, plot, subtext, script, author, receiver and so on, can be understood within a singular context because they can all be defined and unified by their knowledge gap characteristics in the semiological system of knowledge gaps — the language of story, if you will. In this section I intend to show how this unification effect can be used through a representative example within story (the issue of 'genre') and then to show how the same principles might be applied to a wide range of disciplines. My intention is to show that any discipline using a term such as 'narrative' or 'story' can benefit from a formal standardisation that can be used and applied within their own formal context. A singular standardisation provided by a constructivist narratology. Firstly, then, a degree of depth on 'genre'.

5.1.1 Knowledge Gaps and Genre

The term 'genre', is familiar and understood as a noun that refers to the style or category of story or work of art. It is used for marketing by the industry and understood intuitively by the public. However, the formalisation of the term in scholarship and the standardisation of genres in story industries has proven surprisingly difficult. However, it is a term that is relevant to narrative, so what happens if we look at genre through a knowledge gap lens?

Categorising film story genre in retrospect creates a circular argument:

> To take a genre such as the 'Western', analyse it, and list its principal characteristics is to beg the question that we must first isolate the body of films which are 'Westerns'. But they can only be isolated on the basis of the 'principal characteristics' which can only be discovered from the films themselves after they have been isolated (Tudor, 1974, p.135).

There is a chicken and egg effect, whereby both the genre and the story must be present to define the other. And yet expectations are set by terms such as western, gangster movie, screwball comedy or even film noir. Defining the qualities that create the understanding that is implicit to a given genre is another matter. Bordwell suggests several possible approaches:

> Grouping by period or country, (such as American films of the 1930s), by director or star or producer or writer or studio, by technical process (Cinemascope films), by cycle (the 'fallen women' films), by series (the 007 movies), by style (German Expressionism), by structure (narrative), by ideology (Reaganite cinema), by venue ('drive-in movies'), by purpose (home movies), by audience ('teenpix'), by subject or theme (family film, paranoid-politics movies) (Bordwell, 1989, p.148).

However, this appears to broaden and complicate the issue rather than clarify it. For some, it is the film industry itself and its preference for commodity production which brings genres about. Profit is dependent on the successful capture of audience, so success dictates that any winning formula is repeated, and a genre may evolve as a result. For Hodge and Kress it is the audience which knows — and tacitly understands — a genre when they see one, but this angle is also fraught. "Genres only exist in so far as a social group declares and enforces the rules that constitute them" (Hodge and Kress, 1988, p.7), though what those rules might be is not specified. Chandler adds another dimension to the genre discussion: diachronic change:

> As the generic corpus ceaselessly expands, genres (and the relationships between them) change over time; the conventions of each genre shift, new genres and sub-genres emerge and others are 'discontinued' (though note that certain genres seem particularly long-lasting) [...] Each new work within a genre has the potential to influence changes within the genre or perhaps the emergence of new sub-genres (which may later blossom into fully-fledged genres) (Chandler, 1997, p.3).

Kress observes that every genre provides a 'reading position' for readers, a "position constructed by the writer for the 'ideal reader' of the text" (Hodge and Kress, 1988, p.107). Thus, embedded within texts are assumptions about the 'ideal reader', including their attitudes towards the subject matter and often their class, age, gender and ethnicity. Kress defines a genre as "a kind of text that derives its form from the structure of a (frequently repeated) social occasion, with its characteristic participants and their purposes" (Kress, 1988, p.183).

Others, such as Fiske (1987), argue that it is not lived experience that provides the basis for genre, but a text's relationship to other texts within a given genre, consolidating the idea that we develop mental narrative models — scripts — which help us to appreciate the causes and effects of repeated events in everyday life.

> A representation of a car chase only makes sense in relation to all the others we have seen — after all, we are unlikely to have experienced one in reality, and if we did, we would, according to this model, make sense of it by turning it into another text, which we would also understand intertextually, in terms of what we have seen so often on our screens. There is then a cultural knowledge of the concept 'car chase' that any one text is a prospectus for, and that is used by the viewer to decode it, and by the producer to encode it (Fiske, 1987, p.115).

This suggests that the intuitive, subjective understanding of genre is part of a psychological process that defies objective definition. The answer to the question 'what is genre?' is likely to lie more in the psychology of the spectator than in film-making and storytelling. This assertion becomes all the more credible if the additional question is posed: Is it possible to produce texts which are independent of established genres? According to Derrida (1981, p.61), "a text cannot belong to no genre. [...] Every text participates in one or several genres, there is no genre-less text."

I feel sure you get my point. Like many other things related to narrative and story, objective formalisation proves challenging. Authorities attempt to find objective, information-based criteria to quantify a story's empirical characteristics: Hollywood film; Hitchcock film; Cinemascope film; James Bond film; Horror film — it is all part of the drive to encapsulate the narrative context, not the story, and pays no heed to the aim of the author or the mental dynamics of the receiver.

What happens if we extend out of the information domain and begin to think about what goes on in knowledge terms?

Interpreting a signifier is implicitly opening a gap by interrogating the incoming sensory information and then filling it with knowledge from the receiver's process. The gap triggers the mental activity that we call interpretation. Given that any story of substance or duration has many hundreds — perhaps thousands — of knowledge gaps, if you can imagine these represented as a scatter graph, it can be appreciated that every story has a unique knowledge gap 'fingerprint'.

The scatter graphs of knowledge gaps and their distribution reveal patterns and trends that could potentially distinguish each film by type. For example, a broader investigation of a greater number of films could find, for example, that a predominance of revelation category gaps, combined with a predominance of hermeneutic questions (characteristics of *The Big Sleep*) characterises detective stories (and could distinguish a mystery genre). The predominance of privilege category gaps accompanied by a predominance of hermeneutic questions could be found to characterise suspense. A predominance of incongruity or superiority gaps would be indicative of a comedy film. Further work will need to be done but given the problems scholarship has had in formalising genre it would seem further study into the link between knowledge gaps and genre patterns might be beneficial. I have no proof that scatter commonalities would provide definitive genre definitions, but hopefully you get the point. It becomes even more compelling when one looks at genre at the moment of interpretation.

Knowledge Gaps and Semiotics

Alastair Fowler (1989, p.216) suggests that "communication is impossible without the agreed codes of genre", implying that a definition of genre can be found in semiotics. You will remember that as soon as a communication of any sort begins, the receiver automatically loads up a phenomenological context in mind.

If I talk about flowers and you are a funeral director, we both load up a context for our conversation, and the flowers have a meaning in that context. If I talk about flowers and you are a landscape gardener, we both load up a context for our conversation and the flowers have a meaning in that context. In each case, both sides in the communication have sufficient cultural knowledge and experience to load up the appropriate phenomenological context for the communication to have the right meaning. The context that is loaded unifies the speakers and allows them to understand one another and create the right narratives (run the right scripts) to get the desired outcomes.

The phenomenological frame that is loaded up is a unifying context that will help the communication to make sense. A genre definition is the same thing. It is set of signifiers, significations and narrafications shared by the receivers of signs accepted as members of the set that composes the contextual frame. If that phenomenological framing is similar for a majority of receivers, we have a genre definition.

A minimal quantity of information (in the form of signs assaulting the senses of the receiver) inspires a significant amount of knowledge in mind through the receiver providing the framing into which the incoming interpreted information will be contextualised. A Hitchcock film; a Bond movie; a Looney Tunes cartoon; a Western... each could be considered a genre if a compelling number of people fill a knowledge gap by loading (roughly) the same knowledge context from (roughly) the same minimal information arriving. Framing in mind is effectively a genre definition that contextualises the communication. A gap is opened by the genre proposal and filled by the phenomenological context. Developing a method through which the knowledge gaps that are opened and/or filled by the genre trigger information could, potentially, define a means of formalising 'genre'. I am not saying this is a certainty; the main point is to show just how enlightening a knowledge gap view is on just about anything to do with narrative and story.

Broader Application

Genre is one example whereby an approach from the constructivist knowledge context rather than the structuralist information context provides two potential benefits. Firstly, the approach provides for a consistent formalisation through an applicable standard for method, metrics and meaning. Secondly, if knowledge gaps are used more broadly, then the standards, method and metrics can be used to formalise knowledge gaps in other narrative environments.

Let me give you a couple of examples. If a surgeon came to a traditional narratologist and said: 'We would like to define our surgical procedure in the form of a narrative to help patients to understand their situation, the system and the process of which they are part.'

A traditional narratologist would answer: 'OK. No problem. Give me the proven text of an existing surgical procedure, and we'll apply the structural dynamics inherent in that one to this new one you want.'

Clearly, this is not particularly useful. The surgeons will need to have done the job at least once already for the narratologists to extract the structural imperatives inherent in the existing known-good procedure so that they can re-hash it for the target process, then hand it back to the surgeons in the new form. Clearly, the surgeons can do this for themselves. They already did.

Now take a different narratological starting position, using knowledge gaps. We begin with the patient and their mindset and the surgeon and their mindset and we question them to establish what knowledge each of them has, and what each does not have, and we identify the gaps between these sets of knowledge. A narrative can then be created that fills these gaps. Instead of a 'doctor/patient' (superior/inferior) dynamic, it becomes a matter of people sharing their stories to empower each other through gap-filling. It is still a process, so can be proceduralised for general application, and refined over time as more knowledge is added from both sides, and yet it is personal and tailored to the individual patient and surgeon every time the process is run.

I recently spoke at a conference on *Narrative and Metaphor in Education* and contributed to a subsequent authoritative work of the same name (Hanne & Kaal, 2018). Teachers have known for a long time that narrative is a fine tool for teaching but have not formally understood how to structure stories to gain predictable pedagogical results. This means they are unable to structure purpose-built narratives that can teach with known, predictable outcomes and with manageable affect. Some narratives work well, others do not. Using the findings in my research, it can be shown that a narration that includes knowledge gaps can be designed to deliver the teaching. Knowledge gaps can be set within a dramatic context in which the question is raised along the lines of 'how will this be resolved to a desired outcome for the protagonist?' If the answer that fills the knowledge gaps delivers the lesson that it is to be learned then narration can be seen to deliver the education to optimal effect. The earlier instance whereby children learned the Heimlich manoeuvre from absorbing the story of *Mrs Doubtfire* or *Spongebob Squarepants* is a fine example.

I argue that the ability to start with the players and establish their knowledge profile, from the inside-out in any discipline, is a strong validation of the knowledge gap approach. As demonstrated with the surgeon/patient 'shared stories' example, the approach cannot help but be relevant and it cannot help but turn information-based narrative into personalised, knowledge-based meaning-in-story-form. The subject-specific type and form of the knowledge that becomes the substance of their story is, in any context, a major reason why a narratology based on knowledge gaps can be generalised to human endeavour and is therefore a significant improvement over an approach based on structure and information.

The uses or applications of narrative can be formalised using knowledge gaps as part of discipline-specific internal epistemology. Knowledge gaps can be used in the same way across the board, with methods and definitions applicable and understood across all.

5.1.2 Story Industries

When applied purely to story theory, a knowledge gap approach provides for a similarly focussed and holistic definition. Returning to Roland Barthes rather wonderful description of story as a "galaxy of signifiers [...] forming 'nebulae' of signifieds" (Barthes, 1990, pp.4-8), and extending the definition to include a cosmos of storifications, a story can be seen as a four-dimensional galaxy, with myriad routes through time and space. The structural formula derived from existing texts and prescribed by contemporary story advice is but one route through this galaxy. It is a proven route which has worked on many occasions, however its rigid assertion denies the possibilities that lie in new and alternative journeys through the galaxy.

A knowledge gap approach begins with the creative process, allowing the originator of a story to begin anywhere and take whichever route through the galaxy matches their inspiration and the actions and behaviours of their characters. It does, of course, generate a structure, but that structure is a *consequence* of creation, not a prerequisite or a driver for it. A knowledge gap approach is unavoidable, because all stories are made from knowledge gaps. Nobody is forced to use them but all writers are inevitably going to use them so an understanding of knowledge gaps in story is an understanding of the craft. This is why in my commercial work I refer to knowledge gaps in terms of *the primary colours of story*. Like the primary colours in art, they are unavoidable and function as they do irrespective of the artist's actions or desires. Visual art is a function of the primary colours, but the artist's work is not driven or bent by them. The artist's inspiration is not limited nor their creativity harmed by knowledge of the primary colours. Knowledge gaps are the substance of story but understanding knowledge gaps is not going to define the route the writer takes through the galaxy. An understanding of knowledge gaps empowers the creator of a story without colouring their art.

The main value I find in understanding story theory in my commercial work is in problem solving. An ability to analyse a story in technical terms that define it helps to identify the source of the nagging doubts. You will appreciate that this is after the event in terms of the initial burst of creativity. The story comes from the heart, the analysis from the head. I argue that advice for storytellers should be separated from their stories. Story gurus should understand knowledge gaps and how they work, and through teaching these, deliver mastery of story dynamics. (Perhaps this should be called Narratology...) The craft of story is the understanding of the systems and modes of knowledge gaps, so a 'knowing' storyteller is one who understands how they are deploying and working with the many different types of knowledge gaps that are surely present in their stories. The guru does not need to know how the author's story goes, nor give advice on how it 'should' go. That is down to the story creator, who can be taught knowledge gap principles and be left to apply them as they see fit. Stories are about knowledge, not information, so storytellers should simply write stories and then, once that is done, they (or some media-specific expert) can adapt them into a specific information stream that delivers the knowledge gaps in the most entertaining and effective way the medium facilitates.

6 Reflection and Conclusions

As a receiver absorbs a narration, the author is not present. His or her motivation and integrity are not knowable and we are left with only the information stream. And yet the knowledge-role the author has is absolutely present and alive in the communication with the receiver. The receiver may be alone with the text, but without the author the text would not be there and without the author's skilful work, the story would not be constructed as a phenomenological entity in the receiver's mind. The power to grip and engage, inform, entertain and teach life lessons comes from the author. Their presence is active in the narration and experienced as the 'determinate illusion' (Macherey, 1966, p.69) which transmutes, as if by magic, from a carefully crafted puzzle made from fiction into forms of meaning and knowledge in the mind of the receiver.

The clarion call of this book is for narratology to embrace the mind and the story as well as the text and the narrative. I have shown how narratology is poorly situated in this mind-to-mind knowledge transfer that defines story. I feel sure that narratologists have always set out to embrace everything about story and narrative, but we have fallen short. We have embraced narrative and information but not knowledge and story. Narratology is the study of the systems and modes of narrative; and limiting the scope in this way completely misses the story.

Equally, there will be narratologists out there who argue that things are fine. Narratology studies narrative. Narrative is objective. Information is tangible. We are not — and do not want to be — psychologists. Story is deliberately excluded from the formal scope of narratology because story is not narrative. However, there is also evident frustration with the discipline's shortcomings along the lines expressed by Thomas Pavel that the exclusion of story is also the exclusion of the human heart. Narratology is the equivalent of a deep study of skeletons in search of the substance of genius, stridently justified by the certainty that every genius has a skeleton. The logic goes that every story is spawned in the mind of the receiver from the structure in the text that contains it. I argue that this starting point is where the frustration has its roots.

The profound recognition for me is that story and narrative are distinctly separate and need to be understood as such. Story is about the intelligence and activities of the mind that link the author to a receiver; a process in which the text is merely a means of facilitating the communication. The text is essential, of course, but it is just the conduit. It has nothing to do with the knowledge transfer any more than a telephone is part of a conversation.

For me, narratology cannot be complete if it excludes story, and yet this is where we are. If narratologists intend to include story in their work as well as narrative (and I feel sure we do) we need to accept change. In academic terms, this is a shift from structuralism to constructivism. A recognition that a story involves functions of mind as well as structures of text. A recognition that a narration is a knowledge transfer between an author and a receiver, for which the text is a transitional object. Until this shift to constructivism is accepted, narratology will continue to exist tangentially to story. Just off to one side of the very thing we are all trying to comprehend.

6.1 Where next?

In academic terms, mine is a call for re-centring narratology at the hermeneutic boundary. A re-centring that keeps hold of all the good work that has been done on narrative over the years, but now also includes the story. And the truly ground-breaking aspect of a knowledge gap approach is that it gives us access to critical mental dynamics couched in proprietary narratological terms. We do not have to hand the discipline over to neuroscience and cognitive psychology to make good, practical, applicable sense to the world and to own and manage the expertise specific to our discipline. We are retaining our integrity as narratologists and defining the principles of narrative and story in ways that serve all the right purposes in terms of what narratology is and what it can do for the wider world; a world that uses story and narrative for a multitude of purposes, but for whom narratology does not currently deliver useful principles.

In my early work, I saw knowledge gaps as an interesting relativist perspective, but as my research has deepened, it has become clear that knowledge gaps are the substance of story. They are a *constitutive* absence.

No story exists without knowledge gaps. Story cannot exist without knowledge gaps, because knowledge gaps *cause* a specific hermeneutic reflex that is storification. Knowledge gaps are present in every instance of any type of narrative in any discipline, thereby plaiting together the plurality of demands placed upon narrative as a term that needs a consistent and singular definition for the plurality of demands placed upon it by the broad range of academic and commercial disciplines and applications that use the term: 'story'.

The constructivist approach allows narratology to not only assert its independence as a discipline but also to become the king-pin that unites all uses of the term 'narrative' for all applications of story and all forms of storytelling. A knowledge gap perspective is not relativist; it is fundamental.

6.2 Conclusions

In this book, I have demonstrated that a constructivist approach delivers a narratology that:

a) Embraces every story in any medium, form, genre, age, ethnicity or duration. There are no popular exceptions.
b) Includes the writer and a formalised context for their mental processes at the source of story creation. A narratology which formalises the dynamics of story production.
c) Includes the receiver and a formalised context for their hermeneutic and phenomenological activities. A narratology which formalises the dynamics of the receiver of a story.
d) Asserts story as a communication between an author and a receiver. A narratology which can holistically:

- Identify the source of engagement and intrigue in the story;
- define the structure of the text;
- lever off the content of the story events. That is, identify what the story is about in human/character terms;
- provide consistent tools and methods for analysis.

e) Is inclusive of existing narratological scholarship but broadens the discipline to embrace the neuroscience of story, thereby bringing the discipline completeness. This broadening also has the effect of allowing the findings and principles of narratology to be useful to other disciplines and subject areas, such as medical or political discourse, neuroscience and psychology, life narrative, social sciences and so on.

f) Embraces traditional structuralist imperatives. A knowledge basis retains the integrity of existing narratology in that the traditional narrative focus and principles are included. Any story can be defined by a structure generated using the taxonomy and method described in this book because the knowledge gap types, categories and classifications include equivalents for the traditional structural imperatives of the most common structural forms, such as the Hollywood formula, Aristotle's principles, Russian Formalism, Barthes' five codes or Propp's 31 functions.

g) Provides a workable set of systems and modes, terms and definitions, methodology and epistemology; including a paradigmatic method for case study and content analysis that reveals any story's unique narratological profile, power and engagement.

h) Facilitates a focus on the content of the story rather than the framework that gives the story structure. As exemplified in the examination of the main plotlines of *Some Like it Hot* and *The Big Sleep*, the storifications are revealing of the intent, the morality and ideology of the story as distinct from the narrative structure.

In extending the narratological focus to include the story as well as the narration, I argue that narratology becomes more cohesive in itself; more meaningful and relevant to related disciplines; better situated in terms of research methods and formalisation; and more usable and applicable for commercial story industries in the real world.

7   Glossary of Terms

This glossary is intended to help with contextual understanding in terms of the epistemological framing.

Connotation: Deriving knowledge in mind that is abstracted from the denoted meaning of information through the overlay of signification. Thus 'rose' signifies 'romance', not 'plant'. (See denotation.)

Denotation: An unambiguous relationship between information and the knowledge it triggers into mind. Thus, 'rose' denotes 'plant'. (See connotation.)

Diegesis: The diegesis is the formally narrated component of the narration. The text itself, delivered via a form of narrator. Conceptually it is also used to refer to the period of immersion in the story world for the receiver.

Fabula: All possible interpretations of the material that composes the narration. The story is the personal fabula — a subset of the fabula. (See also syuzhet.)

Genre: Categories of story, grouped by common criteria.

Hermeneutics: The study of interpretation.

Hermeneutic Boundary: The point at which information in the outside world, through stimulating the human senses, converts into knowledge in mind.

Information: Stimulation to the human senses.

Knowledge: Phenomenological representations of information converted into human causal logic in mind.

Mimesis: The component of a narration in which the characters live out the real-time events in their story world.

Narrative: An event or series of events that includes change-over-time.

Narration: A real-time telling of a narrative. It is only meaningful if there is a human receiver to experience it.

Narrafication: The readerly conversion of the information contained in a narration into knowledge in mind as a result of receiving a narration. Narrafication adds the diachronic dimension (change over time) to the principles of signs and significations.

Paradigmatic: Pertaining to signified meaning within a given (syntagmatic) context. For example, the rule base that defines a Hollywood formula film story is a syntagmatic model. Any particular film is adjudged to be a Hollywood film (a valid paradigmatic model) if it obeys the rules.

Paratext: All contributions to a narration that are not within the diegesis.

Phenomena: Structures of meaning in mind which comprise a system of signs, significations, narrafications and storifications. A mental representation of experience.

Plot: An arrangement of selected syuzhet information for narration. The narration is the live, real-time delivery; the plot is the planned content for a narration.

Readerly: Barthes term for denoted material. 'Readerly work' links information in the narration to clear and unambiguous knowledge in mind. A shopping list, for example, is readerly, requiring no imagination or intelligence in deriving the associated meaning. (See also 'writerly'.)

Receiver: The audience, spectator, viewer, reader; the person receiving the narration.

Scripts (or 'schemata'): memories in narrative form, laid down in long-term autobiographical memory and available to be used by the owner as mental maps for achieving a predictable outcome from stepping through the steps that comprise the script.

Semiology: The study of signs and symbols.

Sign: The base unit of linguistics comprising a signifier/signified pair.

Signified: The meaning in mind inspired by receiving a signifier.

Signifier: the information component of a sign.

Signification: Signifier + connotated cultural meaning. The second-level meaning of a signifier when cultural significance is added ('rose' means 'romance', not 'plant'. See also connotation.)

Storification = narrafication + connotated cultural meaning. The addition of writerly work to a narrafication, creating a story that is unique to the receiver of the narrafication. (See readerly and writerly.)

Story: A narrative in mind.

Subtext: The knowledge delivered into the story by the receiver of a narration from their own cultural understanding, history and experience.

Syntagmatic: pertaining to the rule base for modelling. For example, the given rule base that defines a Hollywood formula film story is a syntagmatic model. Any particular film is adjudged to be a Hollywood film (a valid paradigm) if it obeys the rules. (See also paradigmatic.)

Syuzhet: All information that could possibly form part of the narration.

Text: The material that comprises the real-time delivery of the diegetic component of a narration when it happens. Although 'text' implies words on paper, it is a generic term. When you sit in a cinema and receive a film screening, you are receiving 'the text'.

Writerly: Barthes term referring to the work done by the receiver of a narration to complete the story. Writerly work requires the receiver to use their intelligence and imagination to project into gaps in the narration and complete the story production in mind using their own input. (See also 'readerly'.)

8 Bibliography

Aristotle, 1996 [~335BC] *Poetics*. Heath, M. E. (ed.) UK: Penguin Books.

Aristotle, Butcher, S. H. & Fergusson, F. 1961. *Aristotle's Poetics*. New York: Hill and Wang.

Baboulene, D. 2010. *The Story Book*. London: Dreamengine Media Ltd.

Baboulene, D., et al. 2018. *You in Motion*. In: Hanne, M., Kaal, A. (Eds.) 2018. *Narrative and Metaphor in Education: Look Both Ways*. Routledge, Taylor and Francis.

Back to the Future (1985) [film]. Director: Robert Zemeckis. Universal. USA.

Bardon, A. 2005. *The Philosophy of Humor in Comedy*. In: Charney, M. (ed.) *Comedy: A Geographic and Historical Guide*. Connecticut, USA: Greenwood Press.

Barthes, R. 1978. *A Lover's Discourse*. New York: Hill and Wang.

Barthes, R. 1957 [2007]. *Mythologies*. Paris, France: Edition de Seuil.

Barthes, R. & Balzac, H. 1990. *S/Z*. Oxford, UK. Blackwell.

Barthes, R. 1968. *The Death of the Author* in: Johnson, P. (Ed.) *Aspen Magazine*; vol.5.

Bell, M. 1986. *Narrative Gaps/Narrative Meaning*. USA: Raritan.

BFI. *Sight and Sound Magazine*. September 2012 Edition. (Decennial poll of critics and directors for the greatest films of all time). London. BFI.

Bordwell, D. 1985a. *Classical Narration*. In: Bordwell, D. S., J. & Thompson, K. (eds.) *The Classical Hollywood Cinema - Film Style and Mode of Production to 1960*. London: Routledge.

Bordwell, D. 1985b. *Narration in the Fiction Film*. Wisconsin, USA: University of Wisconsin Press.

Bordwell, D. 1986. *Classical Hollywood Cinema: Narrational Principles and Procedures*. In: Rosen, P. (ed.) *Narrative, Apparatus, Ideology. A Film Theory Reader*. New York: Columbia University Press.

Bordwell, D. 1989 *Making Meaning: Inference and Rhetoric in the Interpretation of Cinema.* Cambridge, MA: Harvard University Press.

Bordwell, D. 2006. *The Way Hollywood Tells it - Story and Style in Modern Movies.* California, USA: University of California Press.

Bordwell, D., Staiger, J. & Thompson, C. 1985a. *The Classical Hollywood Cinema. Film Style and Mode of Production to 1960.* London, UK: Routledge.

Bower, G. & Morrow, D. 1990. *Mental Models in Narrative Comprehension.* In: *Science* (New Series), Vol. 247, No. 4938 (Jan. 5, 1990), pp. 44-48. USA: American Association for the Advancement of Science.

Branigan, E. 1992. *Narrative Comprehension and Film.* London: Routledge.

Carver, R. 2003. *What We Talk About When We Talk About Love.* London. Vintage.

Chandler, C. 2002. *Nobody's Perfect. Billy Wilder. A Personal Biography.* New York: Schuster & Schuster.

Chandler, D. 1997. *An Introduction to Genre Theory.* [Web page] Available at: http://faculty.washington.edu/farkas/HCDE510-Fall2012/Chandler_genre_theoryDFAnn.pdf. [Accessed February 2018]. University of Washington.

Chandler, R. 1939. *The Big Sleep.* USA Penguin.

Chatman, S. 1978. *Story and Discourse: Narrative Structure in Fiction and Film.* Ithaca: Cornell University Press.

Crotty, M. 1998. *The Foundations of Social Research,* London, Sage.

Damasio, A. 2010. *Self Comes to Mind: Constructing the Conscious Brain.* Random House. Kindle Edition.

Damasio, A. 2011. *Consciousness.* In: The Huffington Post. May 25th 2011.

Derrida, J. 1981. *The Law of Genre.* In: Mitchell, W. E. (ed.) *On Narrative.* Chicago: University of Chicago Press.

Eagleton, T. 2008. *Literary Theory: an Introduction*. London: John Wiley and Sons.

Ebert, R. 1997. *The Big Sleep*. USA: Chicago Sun Tribune.

Ebert, R. 2012. *27 Movies From the Dark Side*. Kansas, USA; Andrews McMeel Publishing.

Field, S. 1979 [1985 revised edition]. *Screenplay: the Foundations of Screenwriting.* New York: Random House.

Fiske, J. 1987. *Television Culture.* London: Routledge.

Fowler, A. 1989. *Genre*. In: Barnouw, E. (ed.) *International Encyclopedia of Communications, Vol. 2.* New York: Oxford University Press.

Genette, G. 1980. *Narrative Discourse - an Essay in Method*. New York: Cornell University Press.

Genette, G. 1997. *Paratexts: Thresholds of Interpretation*. Cambridge, UK: Cambridge University Press.

Gombrich, E. 1994. *The Sense of Order: A Study in the Psychology of Decorative Art*. London: Phaidon.

Gray, J. 2010. *Show Sold Separately: Promos, Spoilers, and Other Media Paratexts*. New York: New York University Press.

Gruner, C. 1997. *The Game of Humor: A Comprehensive Theory of Why We Laugh*. New Jersey: Transaction Publishers.

Hanne, M., Kaal, A. (Eds.) 2018. *Narrative and Metaphor in Education: Look Both Ways*. Routledge, Taylor and Francis.

Haven, K. 2007. *Story Proof: The Science Behind the Startling Power of Story*. Westport, USA: Greenwood Publishing Group.

Hodge, R. & Kress, G. 1988. *Social Semiotics*. Cambridge: Polity.

IMDB. 2018. *The Internet Movie Database*. [Website] Available at < www.imdb.com/> [Accessed 26 April, 2018].

It's a Wonderful Life (1946) [Film]. Directed by Frank Capra. RKO Radio Pictures, USA.

Johnny B Goode (1958) [Song] Chuck Berry, Chess Records, USA.

King, V. 2001. *How to Write a Movie in 21 Days* New York: Harper Row.

Klinger, B. 1997. *Film History Terminable and Interminable. Recovering the Past in Reception Studies.* USA: Screen Magazine.

Kress, G. 1988. *Communication and Culture: An Introduction.* Australia: New South Wales University Press.

Le Carré, J. 1977. *John le Carré: An Interrogation.* Interview with Michael Barber in The New York Times. [WEB PAGE: URL: http://www.nytimes.com/books/99/03/21/specials/lecarre-interrogation.html Accessed January 2018. The New York Times.

Macherey, P. 1966 [1978]. *A Theory of Literary Production.* London, UK. Routledge & Kegan Paul.

Maland, C. 1989. *Chaplin and American Culture: the Evolution of a Star Image.* Princeton, USA: Princeton University Press.

Maslow, A. 1954. *Motivation and personality.* New York: Harper.

McKee, R. 1998. *Story: Substance, Structure, Style and the Principles of Screenwriting.* New York, USA: Methuen Film.

McRaney, D. 2012. *You are Not So Smart.* London: OneWorld Publications.

Meister, J. 2011: *Narratology*, Paragraphs 1, 11. In: Hühn, P. (ed.) *The Living Handbook of Narratology.* Hamburg: Hamburg University. [Web page] http://www.lhn.uni-hamburg.de/article/narratology [view date:11 Feb 2018].

Miller, P. 1991 *Get Published! Get Produced!: A Literary Agent's Tips on How to Sell Your Writing*, Shapolsky Publishers, New York.

Modern Times (1936) [film]. Director: Charlie Chaplin. United Artists. USA.

Morton, L. 1950. *An Interview with George Antheil.* In: Morton, L. (ed.) *Film Music Notes.* New York: National Film Music Council.

Neale, S. & Krutnik, F. 1990. *Popular Film and Television Comedy.* Oxford, UK: Routledge.

Neimark, J. 2004. *Are Recovered Memories Real?* In: *Discover*, Aug. 2004, pp.73-778. Kalmback Publishing, Wisconsin, USA.

Orwell, G. 1945 [2003]. *Animal Farm*. London, UK. Penguin.

Pavel, T. (2017). *My Narratology. An Interview with Thomas Pavel*. In: *Diegesis*. (Interdisciplinary E-Journal for Narrative Research). PDF at: URL: www.diegesis.uni-wuppertal.de/index.php/diegesis/article/view/265/380 [Access date: 27th Feb 2018].

Pinker, S. 1999. *How the Mind Works*. WW Norton & Company.

Pinker, S. 2007. *The Stuff of Thought: Language as a window into human nature*. Viking Press.

Prince, G. 1988. *The Disnarrated*. In: *Style* [Academic Journal] Vol. 22, issue 1, pp.1-8. USA.

Prince, S. 2000. *A New Pot of Gold: Hollywood Under the Electronic Rainbow*. Berkley, USA: University of California Press.

Propp, V. 1928. *Morphology of the Folktale*. USA: The American Folklore Society.

Rumsfeld, D. 2002. *Rum remark wins Rumsfeld an award*. [Web page] Viewed at http://news.bbc.co.uk/1/hi/3254852.stm. [Access date: 27th Feb 2018].

Ryan, M. & Van Alphen, E. (1993). *Narratology*. I. R. Makaryk (ed.). *Encyclopedia of Contemporary Literary Theory. Approaches, Scholars, Terms*. Toronto: U of Toronto P, 110–16.

Saussure, F. 1916 [1983] *Course in General Linguistics.* Bally, C., Sechehaye, A., Riedlinger, A. (Eds.) & Harris, R. (Translator). Chicago, USA: Open Court.

Schank, R. 1991. *The Connoisseur's Guide to the Mind: How we think, How we learn, and what it means to be intelligent*. USA. Summit Books. Quoted in: Haven, K. 2007. *Story Proof: The Science Behind the Startling Power of Story* (p.49). Westport, USA: Greenwood Publishing Group.

Schatz, T. 1981. *Hollywood Genres: Formulas, Filmmaking, and The Studio System*. USA: McGraw Hill.

Schatz, T. 1993. *The New Hollywood*. In: Preacher Collins, A. (ed.) *Film Theory Goes to the Movies*. London: Routledge.

Scheffel, M. 2013. *Narrative Constitution*. In: Hühn, P. (ed.) *The Living Handbook of Narratology*. Hamburg: Hamburg University. [Web page] http://www.lhn.uni-hamburg.de/article/narrative-constitution [view date: 21 August 2018]

Some Like it Hot (1959) [film]. Director: Billy Wilder. United Artists. USA.

Stanislavski, C. (1936) [2015]. *An Actor Prepares*. Aristophanes Press. USA.

Stanzel, F. 1955. *Narrative Situations in the Novel: Tom Jones, Moby-Dick, The Ambassadors, Ulysses*. Bloomington: Indiana University Press.

Sternberg, M. 1978. *Expositional Modes and Temporal Ordering in Fiction*. Baltimore; London, Johns Hopkins University Press.

Stott, A. 2005. *Comedy*. New York: Routledge.

The Big Sleep (1946) [film]. Director: Howard Hawks. Warner Bros. USA.

Thompson, K. 1985. *The Formulation of Classical Style, 1909-28*. In: Bordwell, D. & Staiger, J. (eds.) *The Classical Hollywood Cinema; Film Style & Mode of Production to 1960.* London: Routledge.

Thomson, D. 1997. *The Big Sleep*. London: BFI.

Thurston-Joy, G. 2003. *How Old Is Little Red Riding Hood?: Tales Over Time*. Japan: Journal of Sophia University, Vol.23.

Tomashevsky, B. 1925. *The Thematics*. In: Lemon, L. & Reis, M. (eds.) *Russian Formalist Criticism: Four Essays.* Lincoln: University of Nebraska Press.

Tudor, A. 1974. *Theories of Film*. London: Secker and Warburg/BFI.

Whipps, H. 2008. *How the Hyoid Bone Changed History*. Live Science Magazine. [Web Page] www.livescience.com/7468-hyoid-bone-changed-history.html. View date: 15/02/2018.

Zaltman, G. 2003. *How Customers Think: Essential Insights Into the Mind of the Market*. Boston, Mass. Harvard Business Press.

9 About the Author

David Baboulene is a published author, filmmaker, story consultant, and Ph.D. academic of story theory. His research has provably shifted the cutting edge of narrative theory from a focus on structuralism to an approach based on evolutionary psychology – factors such as knowledge gaps and subtext – that cause stories to exist and to have such power.

Figure 16 - David Baboulene 'A Story Ninja' (Nick Wild, Director)

David is one of the first highly qualified story consultants to also have published works of fiction and film deals for his own stories. He has studied stories back to pre-biblical and Greek times, classical literature as well as talking to big names in contemporary story-telling, including:

Lee Child (20 million Jack Reacher novels sold);

John Sullivan (*Only Fools and Horses; Just Good Friends; Citizen Smith...*);

Willy Russell (*Educating Rita, Blood Brothers, Shirley Valentine...*);

Mark Williams (The Harry Potter films; *101 Dalmatians; Shakespeare in Love...*)

Bob Gale (*Back to the Future* trilogy);

and many others. The conversations with these fine gentlemen feature in *The Story Book* (2010).

In addition to dozens of story consultancy credits, David has written four books on the subject of story theory: *The Story Book* (2010); *Story Theory* (2014); *Story in Mind: A Constructivist Narratology* (2019); and the career defining flagship work: *The Primary Colours of Story* (2019).

Connect with David:

www.baboulene.com

Social Media: @StoryMeBad

Twitter: www.twitter.com/StoryMeBad

Facebook: www.facebook.com/StoryMeBad

There is also a contact facility on the website.

Thank you so much for reading my work. I hope it is helpful.

David Baboulene

Brighton UK

March 2019

www.ingramcontent.com/pod-product-compliance
Lightning Source LLC
Chambersburg PA
CBHW050903160426
43194CB00011B/2266